Healing the Past Using the Secrets of th

QUANTUM TOOLS TO *Help* YOU HEAL YOUR LIFE NOW

LISA A. ROMANO

outskirtspress
DENVER, COLORADO

The opinions expressed in this manuscript are solely the opinions of the author and do not represent the opinions or thoughts of the publisher. The author has represented and warranted full ownership and/or legal right to publish all the materials in this book.

Quantum Tools to Help You Heal Your Life Now
Healing the Past Using the Secrets of the Law of Attraction
All Rights Reserved.
Copyright © 2014 Lisa A. Romano
v1.0 r1.0

Cover Photo © 2014 thinkstockphotos.com. All rights reserved - used with permission.

This book may not be reproduced, transmitted, or stored in whole or in part by any means, including graphic, electronic, or mechanical without the express written consent of the publisher except in the case of brief quotations embodied in critical articles and reviews.

Outskirts Press, Inc.
http://www.outskirtspress.com

ISBN: 978-1-4787-2380-6

Library of Congress Control Number: 2014912759

Outskirts Press and the "OP" logo are trademarks belonging to Outskirts Press, Inc.

PRINTED IN THE UNITED STATES OF AMERICA

TABLE OF CONTENTS

Introduction i
What You Knew Before You Were Born 1
Life—Death—Resurrection The Cycle of Life 2
What You Truly Deserved The Way Your Life
    Was Supposed To Be 3
Healthy Emotional Set Points—Understanding The Absolute
    Attracting Set Points When Your Attracting Point is Love 8
When Your Attracting Point Is Negative 11
Perfectionism—The Lessons of Self Abuse 14
Critical Parenting—Bruising Our Innocent Souls 16
Addiction—Forcing The Physical Body To Feel Good
    Avoiding The Inner Negative Experience of Self 19
Physical Abuse—When You Feel Punished For
    Being Who You Are 22
Sexual Abuse—When Who You Are Is Raped Inside and Out 25
When Homes Do Not Exemplify Unconditional Love 29
Shifting Our Focus 30
Desire For Change and How Understanding
    The Law of Attraction Can Help 31
The Secret Within You 35
The Word Light and The Bible 39
The Pineal Gland-The Seat of The Soul? 44
How You React—Is A Mirror Of Your Past 48
Stuck In The Impossible Negative Loop 50
A Word About Codependency 54
Truth-seekers 63
What Does A Pothole Mean To You? 70

Are You Sick of Potholes Yet?.. 77
Now What? 79
Action 83
Creating Your New Vibrational Blueprint...................................... 88
Creating Building Blocks For Your Business—Your New Life........ 90
Letting Go 101

DEDICATION

Many beings alive today do not know they are not living. To live, one must be aware of and in love with the *Self*. Unfortunately many of us have been programmed to devalue Self—disown Self—suppress Self—and deny Self. Who we are as adults is directly related to the conditioning and programming we received when we were young and impressionable. When our minds were blank, it was then that we were learning the most. It was then that we knew—we knew nothing—and it was then—that what we observed—and perceived through our emotional bodies— we presumed was the way things were supposed to be. It was then that our emotional set points (our attracting points) were being determined. Like a grounding wire—the opinions and values we learned to believe about Self—determined our points of attraction—good or bad.

If you are a being who is struggling to gain control over your life, your emotions and or your relationship with Self or with others—welcome home. In this book you will learn to understand what is at the root of all of your current day dilemmas. You will also learn how to make peace with your past and how to move beyond what has been, so you can truly begin attracting and manifesting the abundance, love and joy you desire as well as deserve. Beginning now—your life is changing. The information you will begin to absorb into your mental body, will eventually pull you out of where you are, and help transport you to where you want to go. In the very near future, you will have shed your old way of thinking, and you will be living in harmony within your being, totally integrated, mind, body and soul.

I dedicate this book to you—my spiritual brothers and sisters—who refuse to give up on the Self. It is this authors deepest desire to assist you on your way to remembering who you truly are. Life is not about creating the Self. The Self is, always was and always shall be. This physical life is about remembering that your Self—is God within. You dear one—are God incarnate. In spite of whatever has been; in spite of whatever you have done or not done—you—at your core—are an extension of the intelligence that created all that is. You at your core—minus any and all mental/emotional attachments you may have—are divine perfection.

Dear One--Remember who you are!

INTRODUCTION

Time doesn't count when you are the child who has been born into a dysfunctional dynamic. Because there is no place to hide, mornings blend into nights. And although the sun always comes out tomorrow, hell never sleeps.

Children born to the self-absorbed learn to believe they are doomed. Worse–children born to dysfunctional caretakers sadly presume their doom is in some way their fault. Unable to acquire the unconditional love they craved as well as deserved—by default children internalize the maternal shallowness they experience emotionally—and thus intellectually formulate a reason for their woes. "It is me," they hear themselves thinking. "I am not enough, and that is why I am not loved."

Every thought a child thinks is first felt in the non-physical realm. Every emotion a being feels is created through the eye of perception. Perception is based on experience. If a child trips, falls and reaches out to his/her mother for comfort and is met with sarcasm, is pushed away and instead is rejected by the parent, the child will internalize this unmet need as a sense of unworthiness. If this pattern is recreated many times throughout the child's lifetime, the child will develop the belief that he/she is unworthy. That 'intense negative emotion' becomes the grounding wire or the emotional set point for that child, and all unconscious future decisions healthy or not—will be made from that point. This 'point' is the child's point of attraction.

If a being has experienced him/herself throughout his/her childhood as unimportant—unworthy—incapable—and alike—as an adult a plethora of unwanted adult situations are likely to occur. Because life is a ride—and beings are creatures of habit—habits of dysfunctional thoughts—keep beings unconsciously attracting the same types of experiences, situations and people, that mirror the ways in which that being experienced him/herself in childhood. Life then is a roller coaster ride full of fear gripping twists, turns, highs and deep lows.

If you were born to parents who were emotionally unavailable in spite of being physically present, due to such things as work-aholism, alcoholism, depression, eating-disorders, narcissism and alike, and you have internalized your parents inability to 'see you emotionally'--and as a result you have lived your life trying to prove your worth to others by denying your needs for the sake of others—until you 'wake' up and bring to the conscious mind that which is unconscious—you will continue to draw to you people, experiences and situations that mirror your feelings of unworthiness.

The Law of Attraction is always in action. It operates on a scale of varying intensities. Emotional set points continually draw to or repel matter (people, circumstances) in the physical environment--*what we call life.* The intensity of a particularly charged emotional set point will determine the rate at which thoughts manifest in the physical environment as matter represented by people, situations, relationship dynamics and alike. The higher the voltage/intensity of an emotional set point, regardless of what side of the emotional spectrum it lies, determines the rate at which manifestation of ones thoughts appear as matter in the physical environment. Fear--intense fear is on one side of the spectrum as intense love and joy are on the other side of the spectrum. Both attract equally as they are each very intense vibrations/frequencies.

If you spend much of your conscious and mental time in intense or moderate joy and love--and you continually find quiet time to meditate and work yourself up to feeling incredibly grateful--and even perhaps cry because you are just so happy to be alive--you are creating great forward moving and expanding energy. And so when you awake in the morning and you notice the sun in the sky and you get goose bumps because you feel its beauty and magnificence--THAT is a manifestation of your joy. When you are the only one in a crowded store that notices the sound of babies laughter--and you smile to yourself--and you feel the joy of the child as well as the mother of the child who is staring lovingly down at her child in a stroller--THAT is a manifestation. When you are the only one that notices the ravishing colors of apples at your grocer--and you smile because you in that moment---think how wonderful it is mother earth can produce such a perfect fruit--THAT feeling that knowing--is a manifestation of your joy vibration.

However, if you are a being who is carrying much emotional trauma from the past, you may tend to feel guarded rather than free. And so, because the filter you perceive life through has been tainted, you may not feel safe enough to let go. As a result you feel the need to be on guard, fearful of the next attack—and thus—rather than notice opulent skies, you are drawn to sights of dead rodents on the side of the road. You don't notice smiling babies in crowded stores and instead find yourself annoyed by fussy children. You are not attracted to the kind and friendly cashier, and instead are drawn to the disgruntled cranky cashier. You don't walk into a room full of people and feel attracted to light hearted conversations. Somehow you continually find yourself surrounded by toxic people and think—"It must be them—The world is crazy—everybody is crazy—life sucks—I hate people."

Because earth is a relative place, time and space are factors. However, thought energy is no different than sound energy that is carried on waves--that manifest within our auditory nerves and our brain processes. Thought energy is no different than light energy or magnetic energy. Although scientists have yet to discover a tangible way to measure thought energy--it is as real as magnetic energy, although the human eye can 'see' neither.

What will you gain by reading this book?

In this book you will learn to piece together that which **was**—to that which **is**—and you will eventually learn to transcend what has been—so you can learn to be all that you were meant to be.

You did not come into this life experience to tolerate your existence. And although for most beings this is their presumed fate—it is a lie.

Many of your questions will be answered in this book. You will learn much about why you feel the way you do—and many of your old emotional memories will be triggered. For some of you, the intent woven into the words you are about to read will resonate within you so deeply, that you may weep while reading this book. If this occurs, welcome the tears. Weeping is the way we wash our emotional bodies.

Some of you may be reading this book because you want desperately to understand a family member or someone you love more deeply. Perhaps you know a wounded adult child from a dysfunctional home and you wish to help facilitate their personal growth. I caution you, if this is your intent. While it is very well intended and admirable if this is your desire—the truth is—only the being, which is in pain—can unlock the door that lies within, that holds behind it—all the sorrow that needs to be unleashed and released. But—it is also true—that behind that door—resides all the power that being will ever need to create a splendiferous life.

You will learn to understand that you have a choice. Perhaps up until this moment in time you presumed you were a victim—and did not have the right to make your own decisions. Perhaps you now know nothing about options and your childhood programming has conditioned you to unconsciously presume that choices, options, wants, needs, and desires are rights that belong to others—and not you. If this resonates within your being—you will ultimately learn—that that too—is a lie.

Welcome to the threshold of your new abundant life.

WHAT YOU KNEW BEFORE YOU WERE BORN

Back when you were a fetus and your cells were dividing rapidly, your tiny being was swaddled in deliciousness. There was no clock to punch and no job that had to get done. Your being—the essence of you—was content just ***being***. You didn't have to ponder thought. There was no need to smile for anyone else's pleasure but your own. If you were tired—you napped. And if you were a little excited—you stretched—and bounced—and kicked ferociously if you felt the need to. It was a miraculous time—and your inner being felt whole and in alignment with all that was.

While in utero—there was no need to prove your self—or to smile on cue. You knew nothing of needing to please anyone but yourself—and the idea of handing your right to 'be'--over to someone else was completely foreign. Your experience of self was congruent and contented. The womb was your universe and your stage—and your being needed to question *nothing*.

LIFE–DEATH–RESURRECTION
THE CYCLE OF LIFE

Exiting the womb you passed through a transfer station—and entered into *another* universe/dimension—one in which would require you to process your senses in relation to others—which included a family system—societal system—ecological—geographical--and socioeconomic system. Eyes opened, your being would be required to process sights, sounds, tactile stimuli, taste, and smells. The world you entered was very unlike the universe you left. Here, in this time space reality—your being suddenly knew *confusion*. Born—you were pulled, stretched, poked, and experienced for the first time—**'light'**—loud noises--external touch—chilled skin—taste—and the breathing of oxygen.

No longer a self-sustaining being—the tiny innocent creature you were—now relied on many others to ensure your existence. In spite of your supreme vulnerability your inner being never questioned its right to have his/her needs filled. In alignment with Self/Source—you allowed your internal guidance system (instincts—emotions) to prompt you. You did not censor yourself or feel shame when your belly signaled it needed food. You did not question or doubt self—when your diaper was wet. You did not tone yourself down when you felt the need to be hugged. When you were born, you knew you were worthy. From your perception of Self—you dear one were supreme—and rightfully so.

WHAT YOU TRULY DESERVED
THE WAY YOUR LIFE WAS SUPPOSED TO BE

Every being born is a divine creation and an extension or creation of *source*. There are as many 'names' for source as there are individual perceptions of that which we refer to as the creator of all that is. It is irrelevant what we prefer to label creator. All that is necessary is an understanding—that—that which you *are*—is a physical manifestation of creator. Your very existence—regardless of how you perceive your existence at present time—is a product of source.

You—**you** at your core—before you were born into dysfunction—were divine and you felt it. In fact—it is all you knew.

And although you might not feel all that divine right now—you—you at your core—minus all the negativity in your life—are still a divine being.

If you were born to two enlightened, well-adjusted, self reliant, fair and open- minded thinkers—your connection to source—and to the essence of you would have been encouraged. As you grew—your needs would have been met with a sense that who you were, was important. Your caretakers would have understood your demanding infantile needs and your inner being would have perceived this new life experience as non-threatening. As you grew and your understanding of this time space reality expanded, your need to feel separate and powerful—would have been met only with understanding. You would not have been shamed for needing to master your autonomy. Instead you would have been encouraged to explore and to challenge your caretakers and your environment as well as your own being.

Into the toddler years, as you experimented and perhaps frustrated your caretakers, the way in which you were disciplined would have been perceived by you as fair, and without shame or guilt. The discipline would have fit the behavior and you would have learned that although your behavior may have been inappropriate according to your families specific set of norms—you—you—as a being was still very much appropriate.

As a young school aged child, your natural sense of wonder would have been welcomed. Your fantasy like thinking would have been met with approval, rather than shame. Your creative mind would have blossomed, and as you grew, and attended school, you would have been able to integrate smoothly—because your perception of self was good. Because you bore within you no reason to judge yourself too harshly, you did not judge others—and instead you were able to stay connected to the true essence of who you were. And if you met others who disapproved of you—you would quickly presume it was they who had the issue and not you. Because your emotional set point (vibrational set point or your frequency) or your perception of self was not one of insecurity—you would have naturally and without much thought at all—gravitated AWAY from beings who tried to pull you out of alignment rather than gravitated towards them or allowed their negativity to take residence within your mental, emotional or physical body.

Into your teenage years, because your connection to higher self had been fanned so vehemently as a younger child, as you gained a greater understanding of how the society you were born into worked—you would have been able to be _in_ the world—and not _of_ the world. Although many of your friends may have been doing things to harm themselves, you would have a natural aversion to drugs, alcohol, or to anything that would dishonor you and your physical vehicle—your divine spirits temple--your human body.

Whatever your unique talents were, as a teenager you would have felt drawn to explore those talents greatly. If dancing resonated with you, as a teenager you would have enrolled in dance classes, or perhaps by now might even be teaching a younger child's dance class. If you loved to draw, or paint, or write, by this time you would have a room full of paintings, or books full of drawings, or you would be enrolled in a creative writing class. All the data that you gathered along your life's path thus far would have innately magnetized you to focus upon those things that brought you the most pleasure—because your connection to self/source was never pulled out of alignment. It would have been innate for you to stay in a positive flow of energy—rather than pinch yourself off from streams of emotional abundance.

Nearing the end of high school, by now you may have discovered what it feels like to be attracted to another human being in a sexual way. And because your connection to higher self has been fostered, you are full of self-esteem. Your attraction to others is based on mutual respect. You naturally attract someone, who like you—loves self. You are so used to honoring how you feel—that if the person you felt drawn to ever caused a red flag to be thrown—you would immediately honor that gut impulse of yours—and make the required mental adjustments—and your attraction to this person would end. And on the other hand—if this person reflected a sense of appreciation your way—and lived life very much like you did—your inner being would have felt in alignment with their equally wonderful qualities to your own.

At this point in your life—you would also have somewhat of a clear direction for the rest of your life. By now, you would have learned what feels good and what feels bad. The data you have collected up until this point—will have helped you make decisions that would ultimately lead you towards amazing life experiences. And when life threw you a curve ball—you would have learned to roll with your circumstances—rather than curse them—and wish things were not as they were.

Because emotionally manipulative parents did not raise you, you have a natural solution oriented outlook on the world. You do not overreact—when things do not go as easily as you would have liked them to. You do not presume the victim role. You do not blame your emotions on others—the weather—your boss—your spouse or your children. You have such a strong sense of Self—that when others try to paint themselves as victims—you recognize these energy vampires and move out of their way.

You enjoy feeling content—you enjoy searching out things in your environment that support your feelings of joy—and contentment. It is unnatural for you to want to spend much time at all with others who lack empathy, are mean spirited, criticize you, deceive you, or treat you unfairly. On the verge of adulthood—you have learned to run from dysfunction rather than presume it is your job to rescue others, or to fix them or to be their emotional punching bag. You naturally understand that life is supposed to be fun—and that dysfunctional others—tend to bring dysfunction with them into life experiences. For this reason—there resides within you no compulsion to rescue anyone. Your goal is clear. In this life experience you wish to attract only more and more joy into your life, and your joy is not found in the enabling, or rescuing of others. Your joy is found in you attracting situations, people, careers and experiences that allow for the fullest expression of the magnificent being you are.

Because you love you—your emotional set point is high, and you can only attract circumstances, as well as other beings into your life that are equal to the love you have for Self.

As an adult—because you were so fortunate to have been given such a fair, stable, loving and nurturing foundation for life—you would be tremendously fulfilled in your career—and your mate would be a welcomed compliment to you and your life. You and your mate would have common goals and very similar belief systems. You would be so very much like one another—and because each of you truly—loves who they are—you both revel in the idea that you are involved with someone you not only love—but that you also *like*.

It is easy to trust your mate—because you trust yourself—and you understand that in this universe we are only able to attract what we are. You are love—and so you are able to relax in your relationship—because you trust that you have in fact attracted authentic love into your experience.

HEALTHY EMOTIONAL SET POINTS— UNDERSTANDING THE ABSOLUTE ATTRACTING SET POINTS WHEN YOUR ATTRACTING POINT IS LOVE

If you were really fortunate, you were born to human beings who loved, honored and respected self. Your caretakers would have also given you the sense that they loved, honored and respected one another, the world, as well as humanity. The authorities in your life would have made you feel as if you were part of a whole—rather than like you were a specimen—and as if the world was out to get you. You would have observed tenderness between your caretakers—and when one was upset—the other would have listened, nurtured, and perhaps—from time to time you would have heard the words, "I am sorry," be exchanged.

When you are born to well-adjusted caretakers, rules are fair—communication is direct—words are honored—and you are expected to be responsible and self-reliant. In healthy homes—parents do not enable one another nor do they enable their children. If there is an issue that needs to be confronted—it is brought to the round table—it is discussed—openly—fairly—and future decisions are made out of fair mindedness. The family is not concerned with facades—or with keeping up with the Smith's. What the neighbors think is unimportant. What matters is the authentic vibe of the home—and especially during times of stress.

If you were lucky enough to be born into a family dynamic whose priority was personal dignity—you were blessed enough to have been raised by people who understood the importance of individual integrity.

Being born to caretakers who honor self—who live their lives according to their own internal moral and ethical compass—is like being given a golden ticket. Being raised by such people almost all but guarantees a successful—harmonious—and joyful earthly life experience.

Because all children are what they have observed—if you have observed love in the most authentic forms as a child—you will naturally gravitate towards only more love as an adult. You will welcome fairness—treat your fellow man with equal integrity, and move away from, yet respect those who do not share your beliefs. Because observing this type of character in your caretakers has taught you to trust self—in later life—you are not overly concerned when an advantageous other crosses your path. Your ego is not assaulted when someone else attempts to treat you unfairly—because you have no need to protect your self. There is nothing to protect—because this persons unfairness is a reflection of his/her distrust for self—and not of any weakness he/she sees in you, in your gut—you not only understand this—but you accept it as well.

A functional and healthy home is one that is even keeled. It is not riddled with ups and downs, and the floors are not made of eggshells. There are no elephants in the living room or boogey men hiding under the beds. In well homes the vibe is easy—consistent—dependable—trustable—and if a sudden storm erupts—it is met with a sense of knowing that this is not the norm—and it is more a passing shower than a never ending chain of cataclysmic events. In healthy homes children aren't stuck in emotional limbo's waiting for the other shoe to drop.

Children learn through observing the authorities in their lives. Through consistent repetition, day in and day out—year after year—children learn the rules of the game their family plays by. Children cannot discern healthy rules from unhealthy ones. Children simply become what they observe through their conditioning and ultimate programming. If what a child observes is healthy, then the child's programming and belief systems will be as well. But if what the child observes is dysfunctional, by the same principles—the children of a dysfunctional home will become adults who build their lives on dysfunctional belief systems—and attract to them their dysfunctional thinking equals.

WHEN YOUR ATTRACTING POINT IS NEGATIVE

Everything that we are—is vibrational.

Everything in life that is—is electrically charged.

Physical beings are magnets, and like all other elements of this universe—are continuously attracting to them that which is equal to their emotional set points.

Your unique physical body (your magnet) is charged through the emotional field.

Your emotional field cannot be separated from your mental field.

Both your emotional and mental field are linked directly to your physical body or your physical field. In fact, there is no separating the heart from the mind, or the mind from the body. Each field of a being forms the whole of the being. Each being is a trinity.

Each energy field is intertwined with every other field. What you think with your brain—you will feel in your body—through your emotions.

What you believe in your mental field—affects your emotional field—which is felt either positively or negatively in the physical body (the physical field).

What you think and thus believe about Self on an unconscious level—charges your being with either a negative or positive charge—which is felt in the physical body—which sends out a frequency into the environment—which then lines up with—similarly charged frequencies in your environment—good or bad—wanted or unwanted.

It does not matter so much what you 'hear' your mind saying. It matters only what you unconsciously *feel* and believe about Self—your worth—and how you have been programmed to—perceive—your world. The universe can only respond to your unique emotional set point—conscious or unconscious.

If you have been taught to believe that life is fair—and that people deserve to be treated justly—then you will align with others who—like you—not only hold the same emotional patterning/frequency—but will also treat you fairly.

If you unconsciously distrust others—you will—attract the equivalent energy being (physical—thinking—feeling—emotional human being) into your experience, or you will become that distrustful being.

Because you distrust—you will align with beings, relationships, stories and alike who validate that distrust—by lying to you—by deceiving you—by lying about you—and so on.

You will hear yourself thinking things like, "I knew I couldn't trust him," and be unaware that YOU in fact attracted a distrusting situation and or person into your experience—only because that is your unconscious belief about others—that is based on your childhood learning experiences about others—which is your attracting and thus emotional set point.

You will be unaware that your very unconscious ideas and beliefs—which all carry with them an electrical charge—which hold attracting power—either good or bad—positive or negative—wanted or unwanted—is where your attracting potential actually exists.

Unaware—operating below the level of the conscious mind—is where your attracting potential resides.

Until you take the time and figure out what your TRUE ideas/beliefs/feelings/emotions/frequency/vibrations/electric charge—actually is—you will—like a dog—chase your emotional tail.

You will feel your heart wanting to be loved—but if your belief about self is negative—you will be unable to attract contentment.

Instead you may attract—infatuation—illusive partners who illicit your fairy tale concepts about love—but you will always end up feeling—lonely—anxious—and insecure—because that is your true—unconscious—emotional set point.

If your caretakers were self-absorbed, you were raised by figments of your imagination. Caretakers who are ego-based—who are stuck inside their own heads—who are obsessive and compulsive in their thoughts—who are more concerned with what you see—than how you truly feel—are unaware that their inability to connect to the authentic parts of themselves—creates a wall between them and their children.

Neurotic parents—although perhaps well intended—condition their children to align themselves with fear—insecurity—self doubt—shame—and guilt.

PERFECTIONISM—THE LESSONS OF SELF ABUSE

If your home appeared perfect and that façade came at the expense of ever feeling peaceful—you were conditioned to believe that control is what you should seek on your quest for happiness.

However—your true emotional set point—is insecurity—which carries a negative charge within the energy system of the body, and may be your basic emotional set point.

If you observed the authorities in your life clean, straighten and then complain when a coaster was out of place—or if you observed your parents agitation and understood it was because their day's routine was disrupted by a normal everyday hiccup—you were programmed to seek happiness by controlling things in your environment. And because it is impossible to control anything for the long run that exists outside of you—you have been to taught to live your life chasing your tail—unaware that your belief system surrounding your ideas about happiness are dysfunctional.

Perfectionism is tied to an unconscious need to stay in control—which shuts down the beings ability to have fun—laugh at self—which—as a result--interrupts the beings ability to allow energy to flow freely and positively throughout the beings energy system—creating what is called energy blocks.

A fear of getting in touch with emotions—is at the heart of the need to stay in control. Often times it is the case that perfectionists—fear losing control of their emotions—which they have been conditioned to believe is tied to being seen as weak—which is also linked to losing the approval of others from the outside—which creates insecurity—and thus negative emotional set points.

Perfectionists have learned to link approval to control—and the façade being perfect creates.

Perfectionism is also linked to repressed anger, rage, frustration, depression, sadness and guilt. The perfectionist has been conditioned to believe that if they do all the right things—then all the other people in their lives will praise them—appreciate them—respect them—and validate them. In the mind of the perfectionist—he/she is under the illusion that if he/she does A—then all others should and will do B. The basis of this type of thinking is corrupt—as none of us can truly ever control how or what someone else does—in spite of how we try to manipulate others into doing what we think they should do.

The perfectionist is unaware that they are continually judging others as well as Self—and so when someone they are judging does not return to them the validation and praise they believe they deserve—the perfectionist will then feel victimized. And until these--web like unconscious belief systems are brought to the perfectionists awareness—he/she will sadly create and recreate impossible negative loops within his/her mind—which will send a negative charge throughout the beings energy systems (chakra systems)—which becomes their emotional—attracting set point.

CRITICAL PARENTING—BRUISING OUR INNOCENT SOULS

If your caretakers were overly critical of your performance in school—and if you were often compared to other children or siblings—and if validation was withheld when you did not perform well on an exam or at a sport—or alike—you were conditioned to believe that your worth is tied to performance—and outside of Self.

This concept riddles you with unconscious insecurities—because on a divine level—your inner being knows it can never find true happiness unless happiness of Self is first achieved—and is found within.

And deeper—whenever a being places their ultimate happiness (validation/acceptance) outside of self—in essence—they are placing their ability to feel happiness—into the hands of a temporary human other—which in and of itself creates insecurities within the mental field—because we unconsciously know that others then have the power/control over how we feel about Self—which only reinforces our underlying insecurities—which is responsible for our negative emotional set point.

At any point in time others can die, leave us for someone else, perhaps fire us from our jobs, move away, cheat on us or deceive us.

Rather than creating harmony within—overly critical beings place their ability to create any sense of positive emotions/charge—into the hands of someone else—which is like asking a gorilla to babysit their pet egg.

The unconscious beliefs you learned to believe in as a child—are dysfunctional—and have you chasing your emotional tail. And until you uncover your true beliefs about Self—the world—and your relation to the world and others—you will only be able to keep attracting that which you are on an unconscious emotional level.

In life you will seek validation from outside of yourself—from others—and be unaware that your search for acceptance has been programmed into you by the way you perceived yourself through the eyes of your caretakers. Because children innately crave their parents approval—and because it is innately the divine norm that healthy parents be able to bestow a sense of acceptance upon their children regardless of their performance and behavior—when dysfunctional systems are at play within family dynamics—this very healthy desire by children to feel loved and accepted for who they are within—often times goes awry.

Critical parents sometimes are unaware that their expectations of their children are tied to their own sense of impaired identity. Parents who expect their children to score higher than other children or wish their children to *appear* to be better than other children—in some cases use their children's performance like a trophy. If the child performs well—and receives outward recognition—then the parent feels worthy. It is as if the parent is using the child to gain the acceptance, validation and or approval he/she craves.

When this type of unconscious relating is at play—children do not feel 'seen'. And although they may not be able to articulate what they feel—in their hearts they will feel lost, unworthy, not enough, shame, guilt, insecure—and thus will become a negatively charged physical being (magnet).

They will presume their parents are correct in wanting the best for them—and will at same time wrestle with feeling unworthy. The child chases his/her healthy and normal need for parental acceptance—but has unfortunately been conditioned to *tie performance* to that acceptance. The child then never feels at home in his/her own skin. Mother and father hold the keys to their worthiness—and the being knows that unless he/she is able to meet his/her parent's standards set—he/she is simply not good enough.

Until the wounded being is able to become aware of how he/she has been conditioned to think—and unless this being is able to mourn it—grieve it—accept it—and then let it go—the being will unconsciously continue to posture him/herself up for failure. He/she will become overly critical of self—be unable to let go—fear displeasing others—have a difficult time with having fun—and may lean towards alcohol, marijuana, or other chemicals to help them feel more at home in their own skin.

ADDICTION–FORCING THE PHYSICAL BODY TO FEEL GOOD AVOIDING THE INNER NEGATIVE EXPERIENCE OF SELF

If your caretakers were addicted to anything—including alcohol, prescription drugs, shopping, cars, sports, television, gossip, food, exercise, sex, gambling, diets, their appearance, work, status, fortune, their ego's, or fame—their internal self-absorption was like a wedge between you and them. Although in their minds they may not have been aware that in their internal swamp of mental chatter that they presumed you could not hear—they mistakenly also presumed this disconnect was something you could not feel. Of course you and I both know--they were wrong.

These walls created by distractions—are felt in the child's inner being—in their emotional field—which causes insecurities—self-doubt—and causes the tiny being's electrical (physical being) field to be negatively charged—which will be the foundation for all future encounters—relationships—employment—and alike.

Addiction of any kind puts the addicted into a mental fog. This mental fog, although is unseen—does not go unnoticed. It is felt in the emotional bodies of their loved ones. Although mommy may have been a very successful business woman—if she was having an affair—addicted to anxiety medication—or alike—even though she may have been sitting right next to her child—**she** was **not** there—at least she was not there—100% in the Now—and her children knew it. Even though the laundry may have been done, and the tuition bill may have been paid—she could not have been 'present' in her children's presence

100%--and they knew it—even though they may not have been able to articulate why they felt mommy was not 'there'—they could feel it in their emotional being.

Addictions and distractions split beings. Although a distracted or addicted being may be physically present in one space—their minds and their attention—(the emotional aspect of them) is **NOT** sharing the same physical space. Although mommy or daddy may be smiling, and joking around—their smiles are empty—and their jokes are flat—because their beings are split and sharing spaces far from where their children are physically, mentally and emotionally.

Although physical beings rarely consciously accept the notion that it is possible to be in two or three places at one time, because we are so rooted in the tangible—the fact is—that a parent can be sitting on a couch—physically next to one of his/her children—while his/her mental and emotional attention has time traveled someplace else. It is the gap that exists—between the parent's physical point—and their emotional/mental point—the child 'feels'. This gap *is* the disconnect the child senses—yet cannot name—and ultimately internalizes. The inability to feel connected to the parent—is a sense the child presumes is their fault. The child will presume—he/she is simply unworthy of the 'vibration or feeling of love' he/she innately—and rightfully craves. Sadly from this set point the child being will seek to fill that gap for the rest of his/her life—most often—with things and with people from the outside—because it is from the outside that the being was supposed to be taught that she/he is worthy. And because the parents have missed the mark, the child does not know—not to look outside of self for worthiness.

Because children are more in alignment physically, emotionally and mentally, they are well aware when they are in the company of someone who is not in alignment—and who is faking their emotions—which creates a sense of distrust/confusion--and thus a negatively charged energy blueprint which is the foundation of their unconscious belief systems.

Although children cannot articulate this unease they feel between them and their caretakers—they can feel it within their energy system as some *thing* negative.

Unfortunately this disconnect is one—that over time the child being learns to presume is his/her fault. Because addiction and distraction is never confronted, the disconnection the child feels causes tremendous confusion. The child is then tossed into an internal gap like abyss. This abyss eventually causes energy blocks in the child's emotional being—and in time will manifest as some type of anxiety in the physical body. Because parents who are addicted are also in denial—many times the root cause of the disconnect between the mother and father is never discussed.

The disconnection between parent and child—is then—like a curse—transferred onto the child. The child then mirrors the disconnect within Self—and feels alienated within Self. The child lives his/her life feeling disconnected from Self—lost—and suffers true self-esteem, identity and self worth issues. Because all children become what they have learned to observe—they sadly take on the disconnect and absorb the dynamic in relation to Self.

Until beings are able to make these unconscious thoughts conscious—he/she will be stuck in patterns of impossible negative loops—and will seek escape from the self isolation, often times in unhealthy ways—and sometimes settle for the escape addictive agents are able to provide—as temporary means of escaping the inner disconnect from within.

PHYSICAL ABUSE–
WHEN YOU FEEL PUNISHED FOR BEING WHO YOU ARE

If your caretakers believed that hitting you was an appropriate form of discipline—you were conditioned to fear for your physical safety. When you are a child—you are innately powerless in relation to the authorities in your life—and this is a fact your tiny being is completely aware of. And so—when you are hit—or beaten—there is a tremendous emotional wounding that takes place that is far more extensive than the bruises that show up once the beating is through.

Insecurities—and thus negative energy becomes a constant in your life—as your priorities are based on surviving the abuse.

Fear is a part of your everyday and sadly—becomes the basis of your adult blueprint—which of course creates a negative emotional attracting set point in later life.

When you are beaten as a child—fear consumes your entire being. You are stripped of your personal power---and the essence of who you are—feels raped and cast aside. To be beaten as a child—by a parent he/she loves—whom he/she is supposed to trust—is to attack the innermost innocent facets of that divine being. The child then interprets the violation in many dysfunctional ways. Often times a child internalizes the beating and presumes he/she deserved the punishment.

Because children naturally love their parents and crave feeling in alignment with them—the child will presume many faulty ideas—in search of finding alignment. The child will assume he/she was at fault—and deserved the beating. The child will, tone themselves down by disowning Self—in an attempt to please mother or father—not only to help avoid the beating—but to somehow find that emotional connection and thus feel aligned—worthy and valid with one or both of his/her parents.

Children sometimes seek the alignment they crave through the beating—as on some deep emotional level—the child understands that being beaten makes mommy or daddy happy.

If any of the above dysfunctional, unconscious thought processes and links are at play—until a being becomes conscious of the improper way he/she seeks validation—and inner peace—they will continue to think, behave and make future adult life decisions based on these flawed unconscious ideas.

Unless this being as an adult unlocks the door within that has kept hidden all the dysfunctional belief systems that were programmed into him/her as a child—this adult being will move through life unaware that his/her emotional set point is rooted in fear.

All future decisions large and small will be made *out of fear*—and as a result—fear will continue to show up—in frightening situations—insecure relationships—and anxiety riddled others—which will all only reinforce what the child is experiencing energetically—as a vibrating physical energy being transmitting through his/her unique frequency—his/her unique negative emotional attracting set point.

The decision to marry will *not* be rooted in peace—or in the sense that the relationship he/she is about to embark on will certainly enhance his/her life experience. Below the conscious veil—the being will feel things like—"What if I never find anyone else? I better get married to her/him because he/she puts up with me. I have invested too much to let this relationship go. Nobody is really happy anyway. I will marry him/her and I will change him/her and then everything will be fine. I don't want to be alone anymore."

Future decisions about work will not be chosen from a point of alignment with ones true inner desires. Choices about work will be made from fear around money or around what others might think. An adult who truly dreams of being a veterinarian, might feel pressured to be a police officer because that is what his/her family expects them to do. Fear—whether rooted around matters of money—or out of disappointing the ones they love—will be at the heart of all decisions—until the being learns to open the door within—that holds behind it all of his/her unconscious, electrically charged—emotionally interpreted belief systems.

SEXUAL ABUSE—
WHEN WHO YOU ARE IS RAPED INSIDE AND OUT

An innocent child who has been sexually abused by a parent, an authority figure, or by anyone has been violated on every possible level that comprises the totality of a human being.

There is no facet of a being that is not wounded when sexual abuse is involved.

Children who have had their innocence tarnished by the minds and hands of the supremely dysfunctional, twisted and self-absorbed—experience a range of mind bending emotions—not only while experiencing the abuse—but in many cases—for a lifetime.

Sexual abuse is rooted in fear, more than any other form of abuse. In most cases children are manipulated to believe that if they tell anyone about the abuse they will be abandoned—and possibly not believed. They suffer from feelings of guilt, shame—and wrestle with ideas like—"Why me? Why did he/she abuse me? Maybe I deserved this abuse. Maybe I did something that caused him/her to do this to me. Maybe I am gay. Maybe I am a slut. Maybe I am a whore. Maybe I am unworthy of good things in life," and other severely out of alignment type thoughts

Because sexual abuse is so stigmatizing—the child often feels too ashamed to speak about being touched—or penetrated. Feelings of betrayal, isolation and abandonment compound the shame and guilt, as well as their already enormous sense of powerlessness. The child is a victim. The child feels like a victim. The child's belief system insists he/she is a victim—and if these issues are not addressed—often times sexual abuse survivors enter into adulthood unconsciously perceiving themselves as the victims they once were/have been and truly are.

From this unconscious emotional set point—the unaware adult may believe him or herself as powerless—may not challenge oneself—may give up on projects—or fail to even try to attempt new things that may help teach the being to feel empowered. They may marry looking to be taken care of—only reinforcing their sense of powerlessness. If their unconscious fears are linked to feeling like they might be being taken advantage of—sometimes these beings accuse others of things they are not guilty of—projecting their unconscious fears onto people in their lives.

Sometimes the abused adult child will appear incredibly responsible in their adult life, and in an attempt to cover up those old wounds that made him/her feel like a victim—in some cases the being becomes aggressive—and is seen as a go getter—an over achiever or an incredibly self-reliant being. The fear of needing anyone—in an attempt to thwart having to ever trust another being—causes the wounded being to live behind thick walls of the ego. As the ego attempts to protect the being from ever being attacked or feeling powerless again—relationships with others suffer—as true trust and intimacy cannot be attained.

The being can be caught in an invisible emotional and psychological tug of war.

The being—like all beings—will never be able to squelch his/her innate need to feel worthy and loved by another. But because of his/her fear of feeling powerless—he/she will fear the intimacy required to experience an authentic love relationship with another. True authentic love requires one to release his/her ego so to learn to trust another with the most hidden parts of ones Self. Fear of 'feeling' and 'going back there to those places within that house those wounds' can cause the being to withhold themselves from others—and especially life partners. Fear of intimacy causes emotionally wounded beings to engage others in a cat and mouse type game when it comes to love.

The being will crave love—yet fear it at same time—and thus find themselves caught and feeling like he/she is caught in a tug of war. Until one of the two adults tires of the exhausting hide and seek game of love—the relationship will continue, and be the cause of many present time chaos.

If sexual abuse has not been dealt with appropriately—and the adult child has not yet come into alignment with their innate—divine essence—in later life often times depression, anxiety, panic attacks, sleep disorders, self-abuse and alike become factors that only lead the being further away from who they were born to be. As life progresses--unconscious to what may be at the root of his/her adult dissatisfaction—the unaware being continues to attract that which it knows and unconsciously believes about Self. As days turn into years—time and time again—trouble shows up—only reinforcing the beings unconscious dysfunctional concepts about Self. Unconsciously—feelings of unworthiness and thus powerlessness lay behind the golden door—they have locked so long ago.

It is not an easy thing for a sexually abused being to learn to trust Self. Their life experience has been one of survival. To escape the pain of being so horribly violated—sexually abused children sometimes flee within. Unable to process the unbearable trauma—in some cases children get trapped emotionally within—and are unable to ever feel safe enough to even consider trusting another. Even the emotion of love is terrifying—as love is an emotion that makes us feel. The sexual abuse survivor—fears feeling.

If the sexually abused being does not learn to believe that what happened to him/her is in no way their fault—and if the being does not learn to understand that they are in fact entitled to feel victimized—because they were—while—learning to fan the flames of moving out of identifying oneself as a victim today—the being will have a difficult time finding the inner peace he/she ultimately is entitled to and absolutely deserves.

And as a result—if this identifying oneself as a victim—and thus powerless—is not released—all future experiences will be rooted in fear; fear of feeling vulnerable, like a victim, powerless and alike.

WHEN HOMES DO NOT EXEMPLIFY UNCONDITIONAL LOVE

Dysfunctional families—regardless of the unique dynamic that is at the root of the family's problem all share common traits. All dysfunctional families practice non-assertive communication—meaning—dysfunctional families don't allow the truth to be told. Violations occur—addiction is taking place--hearts get broken—words aim to cripple—truths are ignored--and yet—the no talk rule is in effect.

The authorities in the life of a child—although may be severely dysfunctional—sadly impaired intellectually and emotionally—as well as blatantly abusive—are the ones with the power.

Through repetition and through observation children naturally absorb the rules of their home and presume these dynamics to be the way it is—and unknowingly set out later on in life—with a conditioned set of dysfunctional belief systems which are at the root of all behaviors, choices, and future thoughts.

Quite unfortunately—these negative views about Self, love, money and others—become the emotional set points—and thus attracting points for all that is magnetized into the beings physical reality.

Insecurities—beget—relationships, finances, cars, homes—and lovers that reinforce and or create only more of what the being is emitting emotionally and thus on a vibrational level—through their bodies energy or chakra system—in spite of what their mind hears them saying on the very limited conscious plane.

SHIFTING OUR FOCUS

When we were children *we believed* what we saw and experienced in our homes. And because in a child's mind seeing is believing—if what we saw as children has taught us to believe we are victims—unless we deliberately change how we see Self today—we will go on in life believing in our victimhood—and presume life is meant to be tolerated—rather than created mindfully. We will complain when things go wrong—when people disappoint us—when it rains—when it snows—or when the mail doesn't arrive exactly when we think it should. We will see lack in others as well as in Self—and in the world--and presume people are intentionally seeking to victimize us—because that is the absolute lens we perceive our realities through.

When we beings were children—we were absolutely powerless to a certain degree to the beliefs we adopted as truth. But as adults—possessors of this miraculous thing called **free will**—and *also* as the only master of our innate creative mind—we absolutely have the ability to change how we see Self today—and when we invoke our divine ability to change how we see Self—by deliberately raising our levels of awareness—we shift the paradigm in our favor.

Because all that we are—is only what we believe we are at an unconscious level—all we need to do is—practice the art of consciousness/awareness—and never ever give up seeking our truths about Self—because who you are—at your core—is perfect—pure—divine and spiritual in nature—and is far less physical than you have been taught to believe.

DESIRE FOR CHANGE AND HOW UNDERSTANDING THE LAW OF ATTRACTION CAN HELP

What is Your Desire?

If I were to ask you to clear the clutter from a path so we could walk to the shore, you would first have to see the clutter and the path—and even the shore to be able to follow through with such a task.

But ultimately you would first need the **desire** to do so.

In order to go from an unwanted point in life—to a more desired point in life—your minds eye will need an end goal—or a clear vision of your desire.

Fanning The Flames of Desire

Healing what has been requires desire. It is not enough to want the pain to stop, nor is it enough to haphazardly wish for a wonderful job, love relationship or any other 'thing'.

Your brain needs to be pulled towards a more pleasing end result (vision of how you want things to be).

Your brain needs you to tell it what you want (your end goal), how you want to feel, and what you ultimately wish to experience. Without a clear vision of what you want out of life—it's as if you are shooting an arrow into the sky without knowing where you intend the arrow to land. Life becomes a crapshoot, rather than a deliberate unfolding of those things you truly desire.

If I were to ask you to clear that path so we could walk to the shore—you would have to have the desire to do so in order to complete the task. If I enticed you with a fee--that might enhance your desire—or if I told you we were about to be eaten by ferocious lions—that might also enhance your desire to quickly clear the path.

In order to get started—you will have to harness the power of desire. Without desire—it will be difficult for you to stay committed to the process mastering of Self and thus healing the past--actually is.

The flames of desire can be fanned and intensified. But you will also need to desire to fan the flames of your desire. No one can initiate this desire within you—unless you allow it. Ultimately—no one has ownership over your free will—but you.

The power to live an amazing life is within you. I as an author and Life Coach can help light the way—or perhaps help fan the flames of your own personal desire to help you want more out of your life, but ultimately —only YOU can do what needs to be done to live the life you absolutely, unequivocally came here to live.

And once you begin to integrate this concept—the energy in your being will shift which will cause a positive shift in your emotional field—which will ultimately affect your vibrational/magnetic/attracting set point.

How To Fan The Flames of Desire

When you were a small child, and you really, really wanted something—perhaps a toy—or you wanted to go on a vacation somewhere—you naturally used your divine ability—without even realizing it—to fan the flames of your then desires.

Children are so much more aligned than adults, which is why it is helpful to remember how we naturally aligned ourselves with the things we desired when we were children as we embark on this healing journey as adults.

When we are children we don't hold back. When we want something our whole being gets involved. We think about that toy night and day. We go to bed thinking about it and we go to sleep fantasizing about how great it would be to have that thing we desire. We talk to our friends about our desire. We read up about our desire. We make wishes on stars about our desires—and sometimes we were lucky enough to actually get what we desired.

As adults we have to learn to focus on our desires much more often. And if our desires for a particular outcome are not that strong right now—we need to fan the flames of our desires as often as possible.

- Wake up 30 minutes earlier each day—and don't complain about doing so
- Journal about why you desire a specific outcome
- Write about how your life will change when you get that desired outcome
- Write about why you absolutely MUST achieve this goal
- Write about why you feel you deserve this goal
- Write about how you are going to feel when this goal is achieved

Becoming Goal/Desire Thinking Oriented

Many people want to change. But many people do not want to *have to change* to experience the change they desire.

If this is your mindset—unless you see that clutter—you will continuously scan your environment for another quick get-well scheme. The world is full of workshops, meetings, videos, cd's, conferences, books, websites and alike, that are aimed at helping people heal their pasts, and all are capable of aiding individuals heal from within. But ultimately the power to change can only be harnessed if the being seeking the information begins to comprehend how incredibly powerful they truly are, as the power to change lies within each being born.

Yes—you can heal once and for all—but not unless you are willing to move out of identifying yourself as a victim. You dear one—are divinely powerful—regardless of what has ever been. To heal—you must see what you believe—then choose to change what you believe—if what you believe is dysfunctional and self-limiting.

During your normal everyday routines—take the time to imagine your desire. As you go about your day—allow your being to get caught up imagining what it would feel like to feel free—secure—hopeful—or in a loving relationship—if these are your desires.

You need to visualize that desire with your minds eye so your mind has a clear vision of what you want to achieve in your life.

THE SECRET WITHIN YOU

One of the main reasons for writing this type of a book is to help people understand on a much deeper level, what the heck *The Secret* really is.

While much has been written about *The Law of Attraction*—unfortunately its concept has been twisted and minimalized to the point where logical minded people reject its spouted teachings.

Let's get it straight once and for all.

The Secret is—you attract the sum of your unconscious beliefs, and the Law of Attraction does not play in the conscious realm. The Law of Attraction is being played out in the ethereal or non-physical/spiritual plane—which is the sum of your unconscious belief systems—that were programmed into you when you were the most teachable—and the most able to absorb information when you were a child.

Even the most logical minds would have to admit that thoughts—are non-physical. Our brains do not think. Our belief systems decide how our brain processes stimuli from the environment. But our belief systems—are in fact non-physical.

Love—is non-physical.

Hate—is non-physical.

Fear—is non-physical.

The Law of Attraction is very much like the above emotions, or states of being. Your state of being is non-physical—although it is at the root of what you are attracting physically in your environment. Your emotions—will always come before your behavior. And the way you have been taught to process your emotions—will greatly impact the choices you make or do not make—about your behavior—which greatly impacts what you experience in the physical realm (your environment—your job—your relationships, etc.).

We have all heard the scripture, "As it is in heaven, so shall it be on earth".

What this scripture is really trying to tell us is—'as it is in the ethereal—so shall it be in the physical', or 'as it is in the non-physical—so shall it be in the physical'.

Scripture also reveals, "As a man thinks in his heart so is he".

The bible is loaded with clues and insights to how the universe truly works, but sadly it has been manipulated by denominations in order to carry out particular agendas.

Your internal unconscious dialogue is your point of attraction—and until you die to the old way of thinking—and are resurrected into a new life (new way of thinking) you will continue to attract more of what you are—wanted or unwanted.

The sum of your life up until this point is the result of only one thing—and that one thing is the sum of your unconscious internal beliefs about Self—love—others—money—Self-worth and alike.

There are only two emotions to consider—or—two states of emotional being to consider.

If you are aware of who you are truly—in terms of your non-physical or spiritual nature—then you are rooted in love—and only more things to love can you experience in your environment. Even when there are bumps in the road—as there most certainly will be—your emotional set point is one of positivity—so it will not take you long to be brought back to that higher vibrational state of being.

If however, you have been taught to live in fear—it does not matter what the particular fear is that you are fixated on. It matters only that your beliefs about the world, Self, love and money are fear based. Not only will you live life on high alert—consistently scanning your environment, relationships, self and others for the next attack—when your life hits a bump in the road—it won't matter if the bump is the size of a quarter. You will react—as if the bump was the size of a truck.

Your aim in life is to uncover what your base emotional set point truly is.

It will not matter what your brain hears you saying with your words. Even if you stare out your window each morning and declare verbally, "I love my life," if your true feeling below that declaration is rooted in, "I am so worried I might lose this house that I love," the signal you are emitting is not authentically rooted in love, peace, and contentment.

The law of attraction does not play in the realm of words, and actions. It is a matter of the vibrational nature of your physical being—and your vibrational nature is linked to your energy system—which is ruled by your emotional state of being.

Scripture also reveals that man is created in the image and likeness of creator.

How do we know this to be true?

Because your life is your creation—full of wanted or unwanted things--and until YOU see the light (truth)—die to the old—and choose of your *free will* to resurrect your thoughts to truth about your true personal power—you are little more than a human being living a robotic experience—unaware that all that you are experiencing NOW is the sum of your unconscious beliefs—which are responsible for the frequency your energetic being emits—and thus defines your point of attraction—positive or be it negative.

THE WORD LIGHT AND THE BIBLE

There are innumerable references to the word 'light' in the bible.

Ancient cultures also point to symbols of 'light' in their texts. The halo's we see drawn around ancient beings heads symbolizes enlightenment/truth/light/divinity—which all exist in the non-physical/spiritual/ethereal realm.

For one to be considered enlightened, it must be presumed that at one point the being was NOT enlightened. If we were referring to this person with language—we might also use words like 'asleep' or 'unconscious' to describe the point in time when the being was not enlightened.

If a being is enlightened—we presume that the being is NOW awake—compared to some time in the beings past. To be unenlightened is to view a being as 'in the dark' or 'unaware'.

Throughout our culture we often hear people say things like, "She/he is so in the dark."

And rarely do we stop to take the time and think about what this person is actually saying or implying.

If someone is in the dark, and yet they are awake—where then is this dark place they are insinuating the person is?

Although most beings never break down the conversations they are having—when we do take the time to break down some of the things people say—it is easy to see that the people involved in the conversation are insinuating that the person they are discussing is lost in the darkness that is held within the beings mind.

What does that mean?

That means that most people understand and accept that it is possible to be fully functioning and awake in the physical world—but at same time to be lost in the darkness somewhere in the non-physical, which is the mind. The mind is in fact—non-physical. It cannot be touched. It is a 'thing' that we refer to daily in our lives—but yet fail to ever contemplate the notion that it is non-physical in nature.

The bible is loaded with conversations between people that exemplify similar ideas to the ones people are having today.

If beings just took the time to sit quietly and contemplated some of these ideas—it would be much easier to understand that when the prophets were speaking of 'light' they were referring to being enlightened—and being 'turned on' (like a light bulb) casting light upon our own darkness and or ignorance that is a matter of our non-physical mind.

Any being that is suffering today due to ideas of low self worth—has a mind that is cloaked in darkness—because in reality—the being is sadly ignorant to their true nature—which is divine—and perfect.

Their inner eye has been deceived. Because of their childhood experiences—their inner self seeing eye—lives in the darkness created by the dysfunction of their outer experiences—and until this beings inner light gets turned on—and they begin being able to 'see' themselves as the divine being they really are—this being will stay in the darkness—believe in that darkness—see only darkness outside of self—project that darkness—attract that darkness in his/her outer world—and then—stand adamantly in the self fulfilling loop—unaware—that he/she created the outward experience.

Worse—when that being experiences some sense of lack in their physical environment—they will say things like, "You see—I told you I had bad luck. You see—I told you I was going to lose that contract—I told you I was going to get sick like my mother."

The biblical interpretation of ignorance—is mental darkness.

When Christ says, "I AM the way, the truth and the light," he is saying that he found the way—his instruction is the way—and if you follow his ideas—he will not only light the way for you—but you will discover that YOU are the light as well.

The bible also says, "That the kingdom of heaven is within us all".

Why?

Because the bible was trying to teach us that each being born has the potential to live an abundant life—if they used their free will to come out of their mental darkness—and learned to accept that each soul created—is created in the image and likeness of our creator—which means—that each soul—if he/she accepted how divine they were—could see the 'light'—become enlightened—and put to rest any ideas of unworthiness—regardless of what has been in their physical worlds.

The bible instructs us to 'be in the world and not of the world'.

What does that mean?

That means that the world is a free will zone and it is full of people who may be living in the darkness—who may be creating and drawing to them only more of that darkness—and that YOU have no control of how others think/feel/see self/or in what they create. So your job—is to learn how to be 'in' this world full of beings that are in the darkness—but 'not' of the world of beings that may be walking in the dark.

That means YOU have the choice to believe in the world of darkness—and thus experience the a world of darkness—OR—you have the free will to desire to enlighten Self—wake up Self—and to correct how you see Self—with your all seeing inner eye.

As it is within—so shall it be—and the good news is—YOU get to decide how to see, think, and feel within—if you choose.

Peace is a non-physical experience—so to seek peace through the physical is like trying to squeeze wine out of a rock.

When you wake up and come out of your ignorance of what a rock really is—then you learn to accept that the rock is not capable of delivering unto you—the wine you seek. And then poof—peace arrives.

Did someone hand you peace?

Did the rock give you peace?

No.

Peace was found within you—through your non-physical experience and enlightenment about what a rock really is.

Therefore—peace was always within you. YOU created the peace. Your mind—woke up—saw the light—came out of its non-physical ignorance—and discovered heaven on earth—since you will no longer be wasting your time here on earth—feeling unworthy—because you were never able to fetch wine from a rock.

It all seems so clear to you know.

You did not find peace in kicking wine out of the rock. You found peace by surrendering to the reality of what a rock really is. Surrender—is a non-physical experience.

Happiness is a non-physical experience—and yet millions upon millions of beings are ignorant—or in the dark—about how they go about in search of this non-physical experience referred to as happiness.

THE PINEAL GLAND-THE SEAT OF THE SOUL?

By now you should have some understanding that the Law of Attraction is at play whether you are aware that it is or not. The Law of Attraction is like any law written about in any law book.

The Law of Attraction however—is a law that is being carried out in the non-physical plane. And unless you can wrap your mind around the idea that YOU are more non-physical in nature than you are physical—and that your attracting power is in fact non-physical—applying these natural laws in a deliberate way will be very challenging—if not impossible for you to do.

The pineal gland sits directly in the center of your brain. Not so long ago scientist discovered that micro crystals found on the pineal gland glow.

Our pineal gland is bioluminescent which means it actually 'lights up' the center of our brain when activated.

The problem is—things like fluoride and poor diets hinder our pineal glands ability to glow.

Many ancient mystics and teachers have referred to the pineal gland as the 'third eye'. And they were not kidding.

Dr. Graham Blackwell has discovered that our pineal gland has a very similar structure to our physical eyes, which include rods, and cones.

Scientists today are exploring the ramifications of such discoveries—as one must consider what this all actually means.

If the pineal gland has properties of physical eyes—then doesn't it seem fit to presume the 'third eye' can see?

But what then does it see or can it see?

What could the pineal gland be looking for?

If the pineal gland has properties of physical eyes—then we must presume creator devised this biology for a purpose?

But what purpose?

If you are unable to grasp the idea that you are non-physical—vibrational—spiritual and emotional in nature—it will be difficult for you to comprehend what the pineal gland is looking for. You might be a being 'stuck' in the world of the material and the superficial. You might believe in propaganda—and be rooted in fear. You may fear never having enough money—or fear never being loved. You may fear being worthy of financial wealth—or fear not being worthy of love. You may fear getting cancer—or of flying in an airplane. You may fear aging—or fear swimming in water. You may fear what others think about you—or fear your own past. You may fear your feelings—or fear feeling vulnerable. You may fear not being understood—or fear being seen psychologically.

But if you are able to comprehend the fact that you are more spiritual than you are physical—or more vibrational and thus energetic than you are physical mass—then it will not be so difficult for you to accept what the purpose of the third eye or the pineal gland is.

The pineal gland also secretes melatonin, which is responsible for our sleep cycles. Could it be that the rods and cones of the pineal gland actually act as a projector and movie screen for our dreams?

And if so—and if we understand dreams are non-physical and are creative in nature—as we all understand that are dreams are a reflections of our thoughts—ideas and alike—then one must ask—who then is the director of these creative manifestations we call dreams?

Of course 'we are' the creators of these dreams.

And what about our daydreams? What about the pictures we see inside of our brains? How does our brain see pictures inside of itself, even while we are awake?

Could it be that the pineal gland is the key to our creative potential?

And if our physical realities are the sum of our beliefs about self, self worth, finances, love and alike—and if we 'see' self as a non worthy being—or if we have been taught to 'see' life as something to fear—is what we see—the result of what our pineal gland or our third eye is observing within our non-physical mental reruns of our pasts?

Could it be that our pineal gland has the ability to observe our pasts—and thus our beliefs about self—others—love—money—and alike?

And if a beings pineal gland (third eye) has the misfortune of observing corrupt ideas about the beings self worth—does it not make sense that the being will project the script it is observing from within—and create the sum of its internal beliefs about self through projection— and out into his/her physical world?

If a beings experience with self is negative—and if the pineal gland is in fact a third eye—and if what we are on a vibrational level is what the law of attraction is responding to—then it must be presumed—that the only way the being can experience his/her outer world 95% of the time—will be negative.

If man is as a man thinks—and if mans emotional set point is rooted in fear—which is a negative emotion—that mans attracting point will be negative. And even if that man acquires great wealth—marriage—children and health—in his heart—he will worry about not having enough money—or worry about losing what he has gained. He will not be happily married—because he will have attracted a mate out of fear. And if this man is in good health—he will worry himself to disease—about ever becoming ill in his future. He will work—out of fear. He will love—out of fear. And he will exercise—out of fear.

This man—like most beings—will only appreciate what his physical eyes reveal. And as his life unfolds riddled with anxieties—he will not be able to see—that his anxieties are the result of how his inner eye (third eye/pineal gland) has defined his belief system as either one that is rooted in love or in fear.

HOW YOU REACT—IS A MIRROR OF YOUR PAST

If when you were a child—when your father yelled—you learned to understand a beating came next—your brain—in its attempt to keep you safe—helped you flee pain—perhaps by having you hide whenever you heard your father yell. Hiding was the way in which the survival instincts within you helped you seek relief (pleasure) opposed to pain.

As an adult—you may cower whenever you hear someone raise their voice—because unconsciously you have tracks laid down in your brain that have you wishing to flee when you sense anger in someone. You may revert back to feeling—like a victim—which will cause your subsequent behavior to be acted out from feeling like a victim. Until this clutter is seen—it cannot be cleared—nor can a true vision of a future reality be conjured up within your being—because it will be too preoccupied by the loop of dysfunctional patterning it is stuck in—that was created in childhood and has been reinforced throughout life--due to being unaware.

Sometimes beings have felt so powerless as children, that as adults—whenever they sense criticism—whether constructive or not—their emotional wounds are triggered, which may cause them to overreact to what should have been a minor incident.

Their inner eye has been programmed to see self as a victim.

In this case, the being may have felt so powerless as a child—that unconsciously—as an adult—this beings ego is dressed in full combat gear and ever on guard to go to war. The wounds of this being are so raw—that the slightest hint of sarcasm, criticism, or insult from another will cause an inflammatory emotional response—in an attempt to somehow shield the child within that was once powerless—in an effort to somehow rewrite the past and ultimately thwart feeling like a powerless child and victim in present time.

Unless this being learns to stop looking for attacks—he/she will see and feel them wherever he/she goes. The unconscious clutter from the past will continuously trip the unaware being up. He/she will push others away—lose their jobs—be labeled as whiners—complainers—as abrasive—aggressive—combative—helpless—as trouble makers—pot stirrers and alike—all the while unaware they have created a self fulfilling prophecy.

They will hear others say things to them like, "That is not what I said. You are twisting my words. Why is it so hard to talk to you?" and they will think to themselves, "They are so judgmental—so critical—and so insulting," and then they will believe that they were right for not trusting others. But they will be unaware at how their oversensitivity to wounds of the past—have caused them to see their experiences through a skewed eye. Even when others are well intended—these deeply wounded beings are blanketed by insecurities—and until they can become aware at how they themselves seek out attacks in an attempt to avoid feeling attacked—as a way to never feel like a victim as they once did in childhood—they will create and recreate unnecessary friction in their lives until he/she is able to see the invisible ways of their inflated—well intended egos—as well as to comprehend that all that is happening NOW is the result of a 'blueprint' of a style (pattern) of thought that was learned as a child.

STUCK IN THE IMPOSSIBLE NEGATIVE LOOP

It is normal and quite healthy to come into this physical time space reality we come to understand as our world—craving our parents approval.

In a perfect world our caretakers would have taught us that our worth was a given.

In an ideal situation—our caretakers would have encouraged our connection to Self—and we would have grown feeling deep within—as if the being we were inside was enough. But because this world is a result of all prior wounded generations that have walked this planet before our time arrived to join this human race—most of us are born to beings who carry with them their own individual, unique, unresolved pain.

If a parent delivers a child unto this world—and that parent--him/herself has difficulty with perceiving him/herself as worthy—he/she will pass the same dysfunctional torch down unto his/her innocent newborn—like a curse.

Seeds of War

The seed of war has been planted—as your heart craves unconditional love—your mind has been programmed to believe—you may not be worthy of the unconditional love you crave—because your parents are self absorbed—and fail to appreciate their importance in your life—in terms of how you learn to perceive your self as a worthy being—or not.

Because they are so absorbed in the drama in their heads—whether the drama is related to obsessive compulsive cleaning, gambling, shopping, sex, relationships with other adults—or the distracting agent is chemical—like alcohol—anti depressants—heroine—crack—marijuana and alike—your parent will be unable to mirror back to you a sense of worth—as your parent is too far away and lost—in the darkness of their own mind—and the chaotic world they are attracting—in an attempt to distract them from their own fears of the past.

As years progress—your body will exhibit signs of this disconnect from your source (Higher Self/Spirit/Consciousness/God) in the form of energy interruptions and blocks—we refer to as anxiety.

Conditions on Love=Conditional Self Worth

If as a child you learned that by achieving high test scores you were able to manipulate a sense of approval out of your father or your mother—your brain has tracks that have been laid down within it that have conditioned it to understand that pleasure in the form of paternal approval comes from achieving. Your brain also has tracks laid down within it that cause you to unconsciously fear non-achieving. Your brain is hard wired to fear disapproval—and believes by keeping you stuck in an unconscious loop that causes you to *only* feel worthy when you are achieving—and thus pleasing father or mother or teacher or clergy—it is helping you satisfy your need for approval.

The authority matters not—it is the concept of seeking approval from outside of self that is at the heart of the issue.

That which you deem an accomplishment is unique, as the standard set will reflect your programming and conditioning which is a mirror to what you have been taught to believe and thus understand as an accomplishment based on the ideals you observed as the norm according to your families individual norms.

While it may be considered a super-achieving event when a family's child learns to finally milk a cow, and is able to produce envious amounts of sellable milk from the family's cow—in another family, the standard set would likewise reflect that individual family's set of values.

Another family might operate under an unspoken rule that makes a child feel that unless she is thin, strikingly beautiful and popular—she is unworthy of parental acceptance and validation. A child from the latter type of family may be treated differently than another sibling who meets the family's criteria for approval and worth, if she does not. Although the unspoken restrictions on approval are never brought to the table—and instead they are covert—and 'felt' on an emotional level—is not only sad—the 'not confronting' the unspoken rules—is at the heart of the families dysfunction. Elephants in our living rooms also reside in our heads. Emotionally toyed with children—feel the elephants there—in their homes as well as in their minds—but don't know what to do about them. And so in an effort to live harmoniously within the body—most children assume they are the reason they feel so 'off.' This type of thinking also gets mom and dad off the hook—because on some level—children absolutely need to believe that mother and father know best. If they did not—their lives would 'feel' unsafe.

In the above scenario, the child described may be spoken to in a different tone, or ignored—or her discipline might be more severe than that of her other siblings. Although the specific criteria for worth and approval are never openly discussed—the tone is set—and it is felt on an emotional level. Sadly these patterns get set fairly early on in a families evolution—and get replayed hundreds of times a day—in various obvious as well as innocuous ways.

The saddest thing is—that if you were to ask the emotionally starved child why he/she felt so lost—they may not even be able to tell you why. Because their in a state of learning up until around the age of twelve—children up until that age—will presume—'they' are the reason why they feel the way they do.

These seeds—planted within their tiny minds so early on—provide the blueprint for all future thoughts, ideas, beliefs, and notions about Self—others—their Self in relation to others—as well as their relation to the world.

In the above two scenarios—it matters not what the specific idea of achieving is. However, what is critical is the sense that unless the child is able to attain the norm set by the individual family—the child is unworthy—from the perspective of the child perceiving his/her ideas about worth.

A WORD ABOUT CODEPENDENCY

Codependency, although is very much associated with alcoholism, in fact—is a dynamic evident in all dysfunctional homes.

Codependency is rampant in our society. We are literally born into a codependent societal system.

Human beings are essentially 'consumers' who are brainwashed by advertisers to buy what they have to offer.

Our media system—is geared towards 'programming' its viewers and listeners to purchase not only particular products—but to 'buy into—or adopt' certain ideas—mindsets—and beliefs as well.

From before a human being is even born—his/her parents are inundated with advertisers pushing to have his/her parents 'buy' the products they have to offer.

From before a being ever takes his/her first breath—the race is on to gain some sense of control over the innocent creature being born.

As the child grows—the attempts to sway this little money generating *beings* parents towards purchasing particular clothes and toys never ends.

Millions of parents sit and watch as time and time again advertisers flash thousands of images a day across their boob tubes—in attempts to hijack their minds—with the intent of somehow making the parents feel—that they are not doing enough for the child they love—unless they choose to purchase the products the particular advertisers offer.

The true marketing tool is—emotional manipulation.

Sometimes advertisers will even suggest that their child will not be 'cool' enough—unless they wear the clothes—or play with the toys the particular company has to offer. By manipulating how a parent perceives his/her child—the advertisers—plant the seeds of competition and thus program parents to believe in the measure of worth the company sets—through the brainwashing television truly is.

It is suggested—covertly of course—that a child will be more worthy if the parents ensure that the child has the product the company has to offer—while at same time suggesting that the child will not be as 'worthy' if the products are not purchased.

It is a double edge sword, because as advertisers try and control what the parents ruler of worth should be, in terms of their own child, the advertisers also attempt to suggest that the parents themselves are somehow not as worthy—or competent—or would be better and or smarter parents if they in fact purchased the particular product a company had to offer.

Advertisers call upon psychiatrists and alike to help them understand how to manipulate the fears and natural needs of human beings, in an attempt to use our very instincts against us—in attempts to manipulate our thinking—behavior—and decision making in regards to what products we open our wallets to.

Advertisers as well as religions institutions use the concepts of duality against its members in an effort to manipulate how they perceive what they have to offer.

It brings us right back to how the brain works.

The brain will seek pleasure—in an attempt to avoid pain.

New parents are the perfect demographic—as they are hyper sensitive to the needs of their new child.

It is not difficult to manipulate a mind that is already insecure and riddled with fears of the future and thus unknowns.

And advertising agencies understand this.

Innocent beings born become like pawns or casino chips—and sadly—many parents fall under the veil of illusion—and jump onto the sheep mentality bandwagon—and rarely—use their free will—to stop—and think about what is happening on the inside of their skulls walls.

In most cases the programming works.

Parents buy into the advertising, and join the rat race that has had its rules rigged centuries ago.

The very nature of our society is competitive.

Parents compare the looks of their newborns to other newborns. They compare the intelligence of their child to other children. They compare everything that touches their innocent child from the car seats to the pacifiers to the kinds of shoes the newborns wear.

Unaware parents—can't even see—that they are absorbed by a material world—that is rooted in programming its beings to obsess over what other people think about them—and worse—unaware parents—are unaware that by raising their child in the spirit of competition—they are quite literally brainwashing their children—to believe that they are not enough—unless they are able to somehow gain others approval—by learning to somehow—be one up on others.

Well-intended parents don't even realize that by comparing their children to others they are brainwashing codependent thought processes directly into their child's unconscious mind.

When children hear their parents use racial slurs, or compare what they have monetarily to what another person has—they are infusing the child with the sense that it is right and good to view the world with a critical eye. What is not understood is—by teaching the child to pay attention to what others have—they are also teaching the child to believe that unless they are able to keep up with the façade society has deemed worthy—they themselves will be unworthy.

What is taught is the concept of unconditional love and worthiness.

All the rules the child learns about his/her world and his/her relation to all that is—is taught from the child is born and up until the child is about twelve years old, on the cusp of adolescence. From that point on, the child presumes he/she knows what he/she needs to know—and begins to utilize the belief systems mommy and daddy have programmed into place.

It will matter not what mommy and daddy say to their child. It matters only what mommy and daddy do and have done.

Children become who their parents are on an emotional level. Like it or not.

So if the parents are arrogant outwardly—the truth is—they are arrogant because they are fear based and not because they understand the concepts of unconditional love and acceptance of all beings everywhere regardless of race, creed, religion, or socioeconomic status.

How the parents have taught the child to view others—will be the lens in which the child will eventually use to see Self.

If your parents were critical of themselves, others, your siblings, or one another—the very lens with which you use to perceive your world is corrupt.

The good news is—you're a big girl now—or a big boy now—and as an adult—you have the right and the power to invoke your free will—and to ignite the infinite power within you to change how you see the world—as well as Self.

When you begin to understand that all you are—is the result of how you have been programmed to view the world—and your Self—then you are only a small step away from understanding—that all that you have been taught about the world—and Self has been a big fat lie.

The society you have been born into is rooted in codependency.

It is a society founded on the idea that all the members within—should care—and even obsess about what other people think—about them—about their clothes—about their jobs—about their weight—about their homes—about their spouses—about their children—about their hair—about their age—about the sexuality—about their finances and so on.

The very nature of the way a being is programmed to think—is codependent upon the rules—ideas—concepts—and notions—that have been manipulated by members of an elite group. This group is quite intelligent and understands that in order to guarantee its hold on the masses—it must first infuse the members of its society with fear.

Codependent thinking is fear based.

Codependent society members think thoughts like;

"I have to buy that house, because if I don't I won't feel worthy."

"I know everyone is talking about how much weight I have gained."

"I have to go buy that new diet pill everyone is talking about."

"My child must have those new sneakers."

"I can't wait to make the guys drool when I walk in the door with that girl."

"I can't wait to tell my friends I had sex with the hot guy at the gym."

"I am not pretty enough to get that job."

"I am not smart enough."

"I don't have enough money."

"I will never have the things I want."

The foundation of all the statements above, are rooted in competition and fear.

Rarely does a being think independent thoughts like these;

"I don't care what he/she thinks about where I live. I am comfortable here-it's manageable and I can afford it. So I have less stress to deal with."

"I will lose weight because I want to be healthy and live a long and wonderful life—not because some advertising agency is trying to insinuate that I am not good enough because I don't look like some anorexic model—in an attempt to get me to believe I need their diet product."

"I will buy my child the sneakers I can afford—and explain to my child that advertising is about manipulating how beings see themselves—and that in our home—we won't fall prey to being programmed—and although it might be difficult for him/her to fend off the pressure society has placed on him and his peers—in the long run he/she will understand that our family practices setting our own standards of Self worth—and refuses to place our Self worth outside of Self."

"I don't need to feel good about myself by allowing myself to be manipulated by the idea that I need to prove my manhood to other guys by being with a girl society has deemed 'hot'. I have my own mind, and quite frankly, I want peace in my life. So I am bringing the girl that makes me laugh, and I feel the most relaxed around, because that's more important to me than what a bunch of guys think about me. And if they do have things to say about my date or me it won't matter—because in reality—I know I am going to have a really good time. Not caring what others think is liberating."

"I am done thinking like *'in order to feel good about myself as a woman, I have to sleep with every guy I meet'*. I am done judging my self worth by how 'hot' a guy is. And besides, who wrote the rulebook on what 'hot' looks like anyway? I am not going to allow myself to base how worthy I am by how well I am able to manipulate a man into bed. What man wouldn't sleep with a woman who was willing to offer sex up so freely?

So in reality—it's not me that anyone deems worthy. It's the easy sex that I offer that is so appealing. I have to stop participating in conversations with other women that are centered around any concept that has any of us buying into any idea that has us basing our self worth on how thin we are, what kind of handbag we own, or what men we sleep with. It's time I as a woman start valuing what I think about me, and begin detaching mentally and emotionally about what others think—and from what society has tried to persuade me to believe about where my worth as a woman lies."

"No wonder I feel depressed all the time. All day long I hear this taped recorded message in the back of my mind somewhere telling me that I am not pretty enough, or thin enough, wealthy enough, and that I will never have the things I really want, or the love I want. I have a lack mentality—and then get depressed when lack shows up. I have to start confronting the fact that my blueprint for thinking is corrupt. I have to start understanding that the things that are showing up in my reality are in fact projections of the blueprint my belief systems are. I was never good enough for my parents, and they always complained about how much things cost. My mother always criticized herself, and my dad never really cared to build her up. Their relationship was enabling and argumentative—so its no wonder I doubt my self worth—judge myself—and fear not having enough. I am only working off of the programming I received as a child. I have to start working on changing my belief systems. There must be someone out there who would love me just the way I am. I know I am a great person—and I know that if I focus on loving myself for who I am—then that newfound sense of love will project outward into my environment—and I will not only find more things to love about life—but I know in time I will eventually attract someone to love me for me. It has to happen—because it is law. I can and I will begin creating the reality I want—by dismantling my old belief systems—while at same time do all I can to start creating more healthy beliefs about me."

Who you are today—is the result of all that you have thought up until this moment—and what you have thought up until this moment—is the result of what-- through consistency and repetition—you learned about Self—Love—the world—money—your fellowman—god—and your environment—by observing your caretakers—the authorities in your life—who you—when you were a small child—presumed knew best.

The good news is—no body is really the boss over you—but you.

As an adult—you have the ability to decide what belief systems serve you—and what do not.

Remember—what you believe on an unconscious level—is what you attract on the conscious plane.

You must understand—the key to your recovery does not lie in your conscious mind.

Although the conscious mind must be invoked to carry out the necessary mental rearranging necessary to dismantle old belief systems—the true 'secret' or the real 'key' to your recovery and thus long lasting well being—lies in your unconscious belief systems.

TRUTH-SEEKERS

As I journey along this never ending road to self discovery—I am continuously filled with joy as I discover that all the lessons we beings ever truly needed to live an amazing life—have always been right in front of our eyes.

For centuries great minds have written about how one might find eternal happiness—from Jesus—Buddha—Gandhi—Einstein—Emerson—Socrates—Ben Franklin—Martin Luther--Abe Lincoln and so many more—the secrets to success have always been available.

But--when your blueprint for life has been hijacked—you cannot project and or create well lives. It is impossible.

The good news is—beliefs are just thoughts you have thought about over and over. It is worth mentioning however, that most beliefs are ingrained when a mind is the most absorbable and thus teachable.

When you were a child—*you knew*—you knew nothing.

You knew you were in a state of learning—and so learn—you did—even if what you were learning was wrong—dysfunctional—abusive—and alike.

If you were sexually abused as a child—you may have urges to abuse children today.

Why?

Because that is your programming—your experience—your emotional set point—your jumping off place—your wounded place—your framework for life—self worth or lack of—your ideas of believing you are a victim—which may fuel your urge to victimize so to feel less victimize and more in power or control.

If your concepts about power and control have been blueprinted into you through the vehicle of sexual abuse—then your blueprint has you seeking control by believing that you (possibly) need to victimize a child in order to feel in control.

If your experiences with sex and intimacy have been blueprinted into you through the vehicle of sexual abuse as a child—then the data your brain received while suffering the abuse is corrupt. YOU are not corrupt—the data you received has corrupted your brain. There is a huge difference.

The sexual abuse of a child is not an uncomplicated subject matter and it should not be thought about simplistically. However, I have chosen to use this topic as a means to express a point, and it is not my intent to over simplify or minimize the sexual abuse of anyone—and especially not an innocent child.

But it is worth mentioning—that most beings who abuse children—were abused *as* children.

It is impossible to see *beyond* corrupted screenplays of our internal eye-—if what has corrupted our vision of self and of the world is heinous.

The pangs of childhood become like directors and instruct we the beings—to 'act out' the script that has been pushed upon us by the authorities in our lives.

When we were small innocent children—we had no choices—nor did we have the right to question authority. We absorbed what we observed—unaware at how our internal eye was being blueprinted to believe in a matrix of lies—and illusions.

Wounds remind us that the world is not safe—and so we cling to what we know—and fear too fiercely to consider dropping our armor—and dare to peek above the veil of illusion.

We lack self-confidence to go beyond what our family systems have taught us to believe—even when—what they have taught us—hurts us.

Although we are in pain—it is all we know—and has sadly become our security as well as the roots of our insecurities.

But when we have finally had enough—and our spirits can hold not one more ounce of pain—sometimes frustration forces us to let go.

And when we let go of all that we know—it feels as if we are swimming in an emotional abyss.

But if we hold on—to the idea—that with all that we know gone—we actually have the chance to—begin anew—miraculously--the light at the end of our emotional tunnel—begins to illuminate brightly.

May the words of these truth-seekers of our pasts enlighten you—and support you in the understanding—that—there is so much more to life—than what you presently know.

May you also understand—that beyond the walls of your fears—is a world full of beauty—inspiration—joy—blessings—love—and yes—abundance.

The stream of wellbeing abounds, even in your ignorance of it.

May your hearts open—your energy centers clear—and your mind expand as well as accept that there is much to be grateful for—in spite of what has ever been—a part of your life.

Buddha

"You can search throughout the entire universe for someone who is more deserving of your love and affection than you are yourself, and that person is not to be found anywhere. You, yourself, as much as anybody in the entire universe deserves *your* love and affection"

"No one saves us but ourselves. No one can and no one may. We ourselves must walk the path."

"Work out your own salvation. Do not depend on others."

Abraham Lincoln

"I am not bound to win, but I am bound to be true. I am not bound to succeed, but I am bound to live by the light that I have. I must stand with anybody that stands right, and stand with him while he is right, and part with him when he goes wrong."

"I'm a slow walker, but I never walk back."

Shakespeare

"To thine own self be true, and it must follow, as the night the day, thou canst not then be false to any man."

Aristotle

Cummings

"The hardest challenge is to be yourself in a world where everyone is trying to make you be somebody else."

WHAT DOES A POTHOLE MEAN TO YOU?

Now what? Now that we understand that what you experienced as a child has programmed your beliefs about everything in life—where do we go from here?

Now that we understand that the reason you attract controlling, narcissistic, deceiving women into your life, is because your first experience for love was through your relationship with your mother—who you perceived as domineering, unfair, and emotionally unavailable—what do we do with that understanding?

How do we go from comprehending that your data, which is responsible for your emotional set point, which in actuality—defines your vibrational frequency—positive or negative—to changing what you believe so you can begin experiencing more of what your inner being/spirit/higher self truly deserves?

Now that we understand that you keep attracting men into your life who make fun of you whenever you approach them about your feelings—because your framework for self respect was corrupted long ago—by parents who did not respect one another—nor instilled within you a sense that what you felt emotionally was important or valid—how do you begin altering what you believe on an unconscious level, so that you can begin attracting true abundance into your life?

How do we take this newfound information and use it deliberately to begin changing the direction of our lives?

How do we heal what has been done, in order to create the life we truly desire?

If You Can See It—You Can Change It

Anyone can avoid a pothole while driving, IF they can see it before they actually drive into it.

But—the key is—your brain has to acknowledge what a pothole is—and what it will mean if you drive into one. If your brain does not understand that a pothole can create negative and painful experiences for you and your car—it will not even know to avoid potholes.

Deliberately Altering Your Brains Perceptions of Pain and Pleasure

Let's say you grew up in a home where mom and dad always drove the family car into potholes. Let's say that every time you got in the car with one of your parents, your family car regularly drove into potholes.

Imagine if your family car couldn't drive more than ten feet without hitting a pothole. Imagine if your mother and father never complained about the potholes. Imagine if, no matter how many flat tires your family car endured—your mother and father never associated the flat tires—and all the subsequent inconveniences, mechanic bills, anxiety and alike—with hitting the potholes.

Imagine pulling off the side of the road, and watching dad fix a flat tire on your family car. Imagine being a small child, sitting in the back seat, and watching dad stand outside in a snowstorm, alongside your car, as mom went about talking to him as if nothing was really wrong. Imagine if after changing the flat tire, dad got into the car, and never made mention that the last giant pothole he drove into caused the tire to explode. Imagine if, you and your family rode for another mile, only to have dad drive right into another huge pothole. Imagine if this time, all four tires tore open, and your family was stuck on the highway in the freezing cold. Imagine if you and your family sat there overnight waiting for a tow truck. Imagine if, mom and dad never told you the reason you were all in the chaotic, dangerous situation you were in, was because dad kept driving into potholes.

If your father never associated all of his aggravation over his car with the potholes—he might have blamed his cars tires, the road, your mother, god, or fate for all of his problems instead.

Denial works in this way.

Alcoholics for instance, blame their spouses for complaining about their drinking, rather than understand the complaining they are hearing—is due to their drinking and their behavior as a result of them drinking.

The alcohol is not the problem. The denial about the husband's abuse of alcohol and his behavior is. The wife might complain about alcohol—while the husband complains about the wife's complaining. The real issue is the addiction process—and the denial about the addiction.

But—when your brain associates more pleasure with drinking—than it does with not drinking—it is impossible to choose to stop drinking—without some deliberate conscious decision making. The brain will automatically pull a being towards what it believes can bring it pleasure—and away from what it believes (or has been programmed to believe) will cause it pain.

Because human beings are programmed to look outside of self—rather than within—a being who is 'out of touch' with self—will lack the ability to look within as the reason for why their life is not working and is draped in confusion, chaos, angst, frustration, anger, resentment, jealousy, or poverty.

When life goes haywire—he/she will stay 'of the world' and set their eyes upon the material and illusionary world—and with a blind inner eye—see only the world of the physical—and others in it—and unconsciously believe that others are responsible for why they feel as they do.

Unaware—that their negative set points—and their ignorance of self is the true cause of their dilemma's—beings chase their tails—jump in and out of relationships—or keep attracting relationships that do not serve them—falsely believing that others are the reason they cannot find peace.

If your mother and father rarely if ever looked within for the 'why's to their unhappiness—and instead—just kept doing the next day the very same thing they did the day before—you have not been taught to associate pleasure with soul seeking.

Instead—you have been taught to fixate on things in the material world, and so when life gets bumpy—you do not naturally look within. Instead—you keep thinking the way you have been programmed to think—and falsely believe you have no real control over your happiness.

If you are the child of the pothole loving family, you have been programmed to believe that life is supposed to be filled with potholes, frustration, enormous car bills, chaos, turmoil, dangerous road trips, anxiety, and fear. You might believe that everyone has such terrible life experiences as well.

When you are old enough to buy a car, you will not know to avoid potholes, and in fact, you will be magnetically drawn to them. And when your car hits a pothole, you will not even flinch, because that is your emotional set point. You are comfortable with potholes—because that is your norm. Even though every time you get in your car, you believe you know you might get a flat tire—and even though you know you could get into a terrible car accident if your tire explodes—you get in your car anyway—because you do not know to associate potholes with the fears you experience when getting into your car. You have been programmed to believe life should be endured, not enjoyed. Angst was your family's emotional set point—and now it is yours as well.

Because your parents never taught you to associate the angst your family felt when your car got a flat tire with potholes—you will have no pain associated with the idea of a pothole. Instead, you will feel powerless over the angst—because you might believe that the tires are the problem—and because you need the tires in order for your car to get you where you need to go (pleasure)—you will be unable to avoid potholes—simply because your brain has no wiring associating potholes with flat tires—or potholes with angst.

You will keep on getting into your car and driving right into potholes—because your brain believes it needs your car to get you where you need to go—and that frustration is just part of normal life—because in your family—frustration was a normal part of life.

Now imagine you meet someone at work and they have asked you for a ride home. Imagine if while driving your friend home, he saw a pothole way out in front of your car and yelled at you to 'watch out'. Imagine if your friend actually pushed your steering wheel to the left to avoid the pothole. Imagine if your friend asked you, "Didn't you see that pothole?" Imagine what you would say.

You might say, "What's a pothole?"

You might even be really angry that your friend yelled at you and tried to get you to avoid the pothole.

Imagine if your friend asked, "Why are you so upset? All I did was try to get you to avoid getting a flat tire." Imagine how you'd feel. You might think he was crazy, because flat tires are a part of your normal everyday life. You might be so infuriated that he suggested that flat tires are things that should be avoided. You might call your father and say, "Can you imagine the nerve of this guy, trying to get me to believe that flat tires aren't necessary? He must be nuts. Everybody gets two or three flats a day. He must be living in some kind of fantasy world or something."

Imagine the next day at work. You might ask your friend if he wants another ride home. If your co-worker grew up with parents who taught him to avoid the pain that comes from hitting potholes, he will say something like, "No thank you. Thanks for the offer, but I am going to take the bus home tonight." Because your friend has an association in his brain that has him wired to believe that potholes are--not only the causes of flat tires—but they are also the cause of unnecessary pain, drama, bills, chaos, time lost, and frustration—he will not be attracted to you—or your offer for a ride home.

Imagine you were at the grocery store and you saw an attractive woman who was obviously struggling with bags of groceries, as she was attempting to load them into her car. You don't know why you feel so drawn to her. All you know is you feel a pull towards her. Feeling this incredible attraction, you feel compelled to approach her, and as you do, she wipes sweat from her brow and says, "Oh hello. By any chance do you know a tow truck driver? I blew out my spare tire on the way over here, and I got another flat as I was driving into this parking lot to go grocery shopping. I just moved into the area, so I am not familiar with the tire companies yet."

As she speaks, you feel like the heavens have opened and as if your ship has come in. She is speaking your language, and you feel as if you have found your soul mate—and you're right.

"Why of course I know a tow truck driver. In fact, I know them all", you say, as you beam full of hero like pride. "Why don't you put your groceries in my car? I can drive you home. I have three spare tires in my trunk. It shouldn't take us more than six hours to get you home," you finish off saying, as you notice her eyes begin to swoon. She too feels drawn to you—as you both have similar beliefs about the world.

And as you two drive home in a blizzard, and as you plow your car right into a pothole, you smile as you feel your car begin to clunk due to splitting your tire. Your new girlfriend smiles back and says, "Want me to get the jack?" and you think—"Finally a girl after my own heart."

ARE YOU SICK OF POTHOLES YET?

Imagine it's ten years later, and by now you and your flat tire-accepting girlfriend have married and have a couple of kids. Your tire bills are astronomical. Your new wife gets even more flat tires in a day than you do. You're tired of her complaining about how long it takes you to get home from work. Most of the time she's in bed by the time you get home. Your children are always at the doctor, because they tend to get sick often. The doctor has told you that your children must not spend so much time out in the cold. You're frustrated and at a loss, because you and your family get stuck in the cold all the time because of all the flat tires you seem to experience every time you take the kids out for a drive. You're in danger of losing your job, because you're always late for work. You're frustrated because you keep getting disciplined for being tardy and your work performance is suffering. You keep thinking to yourself, "The world is crazy. They're all out to get me. I am doing everything right."

One late night you're on your third flat tire of the day, and you're stuck on the side of the road waiting for a tow truck to come rescue you. It's a new tow truck driver. You've never met this man before, and as he approaches you shivering in the cold, he says, "You're the seventh guy tonight I have had to rescue because of that huge pothole back there."

Exhausted, frigid, and numb from the cold you remember your co-worker from a decade ago. Suddenly you recall his words, "Didn't you see that pothole?"

You look at the tow truck driver and ask, "What's a pothole?" Curious, he stares at you dumbfounded, and asks, "Are you kidding me buddy?"

You begin to understand, that there is something these two men know that you do not.

"No seriously what's a pothole?" you ask the tow truck driver again. He now understands you really do not know what a pothole is, feels empathy towards you, and begins to describe what a pothole looks like.

You then ask, "Are you saying that all of the flat tires I have experienced throughout my life were because I drove into potholes?" and the driver says, "I am sorry that I am the one telling you this buddy, but yes, all of your flat tires are the result of you driving into potholes. "

You stand there and are immediately sucked back into time. You remember all the nights you sat in your family car shivering as dad and mom changed tire after tire on your car. You remember all the doctor's appointments you had and how sick you used to be because of all the time you spent in your broken down family car. You remember all the nights you tried to stay up in the hopes that you would see your father before falling asleep. You remember all the complaining your father did about the tow truck and tire bills he had to pay. You remember all the times you were late for school, and all the parties you missed because of all the time you spent on the side of the road in your broken down car. And then it hits you. You married your mother, became your father, and your son is a younger version of you.

NOW WHAT?

You get it now. The world is a vibrational universe, *and* it is **indifferent**.

All that you are—is the result of what you have experienced on a vibrational level. If your inner eye sees you as unworthy—then unworthiness is what you have been attracting into your adult life. You will have attracted unworthy conversations—unworthy employment—unworthy friends—and unworthy love interests. Your inner dialogue will have you blaming the world for your unhappiness, and you will be filled with an overall sense of dissatisfaction. Unaware—you might have grown angry, resentful, and untrusting of others. All of these unattended negative emotions—are of course—vibrational in nature. Because the universe is indifferent—and only cares about what vibrational frequency you are emitting—your unconscious emotional set point (your point of attraction)—can only attract its vibrational match.

As wonderful as this news is to some—at same time—it can be a bit disheartening—because—sadly many beings believe in their victimhood—and dig their heels into their victim mentality set point—which is at the root of their dysfunctional, dissatisfying point of attraction—and find it almost impossible to move beyond the veil of illusion—that has them believing they are not divine, worthy, powerful creators.

It is difficult to stay aware of the fact that the universe is indifferent. It is extremely challenging when you are a being who has been savagely brutalized as a child—to remember that the universe cares not what has happened to you—and can only hear what your being is transmitting on a vibrational level.

Beings fail to understand, that whenever they posture themselves as victims—justifiably so or otherwise—they are unknowingly victimizing themselves all over again.

Beings also fail to understand that when they are in business—and their agenda is to 'get over' on another company, and or individual in order to turn a profit—their business point of attraction—is rooted in fear. If deceit is a dynamic that is incorporated into a business relationship—or if any form of denial is webbed into a financial relationship—the attracting point is negative—and one of manipulation. Eventually all parties involved will wind up being and feeling manipulated, and drizzled in fear. It may take a year, or two or three—or maybe ten—but eventually the universe will bring that magnetic attraction right back to its north end, and the vibrational loop will be complete.

Society has you believing in the concept of revenge—anger—victimhood—pay back—retaliation—self-pity—and powerlessness.

Often times—beings are taught to believe in labels. You believe you are destined to be alcoholics—bulimics—sex-aholics—drug addicts—over eaters—adulterers—swindlers—and have not been taught to believe that as a divine being—the only label you deserve is 'I AM'.

You are the great 'I AM' whether you believe you are or not.

You are—(*I AM*) divine, light, love, made in the image of creator, powerful, truth, creative, the way, and the creator of your own reality.

For you to heal, and begin manifesting a life of joy—you must first learn to *believe*.

You must learn to believe in all this book has laid out for you.

You must believe that the universe is vibrational—and indifferent.

You must believe that all that you are—is the result of your unconscious perceptions and emotions—albeit negative or positive.

You must believe that what you have attracted—is the result of your unconscious emotional/vibrational set points.

You must believe you can change your emotional set points.

You must believe that you are worthy of joy.

You must believe it is necessary to let go of believing other people should change so to make your life more pleasing.

You must believe it is your responsibility to create happiness—and is not someone else's.

You must believe it is necessary to release the labels you have adopted and or absorbed about self, which do not serve you.

You must believe it is necessary to rock the boat.

You must believe it is not your job to make others happy or agree or validate you.

You must believe you are enough—and worthy of wonderful life experiences.

You must believe you can change your inner perception of self.

You must believe that all things are possible.

You must believe you were and are created in the image and likeness of creator—and within you—exists the power to create worlds.

ACTION

Yes, you must believe, but even before you can muster up enough strength and resolve to change your beliefs about self—you must learn to fan the flames of desire.

In order to fan the flames of desire—one must acknowledge that happiness in many ways must be your first priority.

What does that mean?

If your dream job was in Japan, but your employer informed you that you would have to learn Japanese in order to land the position, within you would be born a desire to learn Japanese.

If however, you did not believe you could ever learn Japanese—it would be quite a marvelous task for you to learn Japanese.

But, if the desire in you was strong enough to move to Japan for your dream job, then your beliefs might sway more towards the concept of "I think I can", rather than towards, "I know I can't".

Henry Ford said it best, many times over.

"Whether you think you can, or you think you can't--you're right."

"Don't find fault, find a remedy; anybody can complain."

"The only real mistake is the one from which we learn nothing."

"Thinking is the hardest work there is, which is probably the reason so few engage in it."

"It has been my observation that most people get ahead during the time that others waste."

"When everything seems to be going against you, remember that the airplane takes off against the wind, not with it."

"Vision without execution is just hallucination."

"You say I started out with practically nothing, but that isn't correct. We all start with all there is, it's how we use it that makes things possible."

"One of the greatest discoveries a person makes, one of their great surprises, is to find they can do what they were afraid they couldn't do."

"A business absolutely devoted to service will have only one worry about profits. They will be embarrassingly large."

Without action, your desires are pure fantasy. Without execution, your being cannot manifest the thing you think of.

Henry Ford had a desire, vision and belief. All three components are of the ethereal/non-physical. It was not until Ford began putting his desires, vision and beliefs into action—did his thoughts begin to become things.

There is also another factor to consider.

Henry Ford had positive INTENT. His point of attraction was positive, exciting, anticipant, joyful, creative, enthusiastic, hopeful, and jubilant, focused, certain, adrenalized, and intoxicating.

Now imagine YOU are the creator of all that is.

Imagine YOU were the artist that built this universe and all that is.

Imagine YOU created the seas.

Imagine YOU created the sky, the sun, the moon, and the stars.

Imagine YOU were the mastermind behind DNA.

Imagine YOU were the designer that decided how this planets ecosystem would function.

Imagine YOU were the source responsible for this planets food chain.

Imagine YOU were the one that came up with all the ideas necessary to create a magnificent planet that was capable of sustaining itself without human involvement.

Imagine YOU were the architect of planet earth.

Imagine YOU were the one who decided what species of birds would fly where, and what colors their feathers would be.

Imagine YOU were the one who invented color.

Imagine YOU were the one who birthed the concept of a peacock, leopard, zebra, and bumblebees.

Imagine what that would feel like, to be the orchestrator of all that is.

Now take your mind back to Henry Ford.

Imagine if YOU were the man who imagined people traveling in mechanical automobiles rather than traveling by horse.

Imagine YOU were the one who could not get the image of people driving in cars out of your mind—although no one in the world had ever imagined such ideas before.

Imagine if YOU believed you could pull it off.

Imagine if YOU had a burning desire to see your vision come true.

Imagine if YOU had an intense intent to put hungry people to work.

Imagine if YOU not only wanted to build the worlds first car, but you also had the pure intent to help as many people as possible while attempting to make your imagined idea a reality.

How would you feel?

Of course, you would feel excited, anticipant, joyful, creative enthusiastic, hopeful, and jubilant, focused, certain, adrenalized, and intoxicated.

In order to manifest abundance of any kind in this universe, it is first necessary to become as emotionally (vibration-ally) equivalent to that thing you desire.

Henry Ford was excited long before his first car ever rolled onto the pavement.

Henry Ford's emotional set point was so strong magnetically, that the he literally aligned himself with the same type of energy that created this universe.

And the absolute truth is—all men, women and even children—hold within them the same power.

The question one needs to ask oneself is, "What do I believe?" Once you know what your unconscious emotional (vibrational) set point is—then you have the ability to begin putting into action—the types of behaviors that will bring about more positive change in your life.

If all you keep doing is complaining about why your life is the way it is—and you never take the time to look within—to uncover your corrupt data (belief systems)—and if your emotional and thus vibrational set point stays stuck at a negative point of attraction—you can only continue to attract more of the things you hear yourself saying you don't want.

CREATING YOUR NEW VIBRATIONAL BLUEPRINT

All great business ideas need a plan. Your life is your business. In fact, it's no ones else's responsibility to make your life their business.

Begin with a mission statement.

All that is required is a notebook. I prefer marble notebooks, but any solid bound notebook will do.

Write down your intent.

What kind of life do you desire? Where would you like to live? What kind of emotions do you want to experience in a relationship? How do you want to feel on a daily basis? What do you wish to accomplish, and why do you want to accomplish the thing you feel yourself wishing to achieve?

An example of a positive Life's Business Mission Statement

"From this moment forward I promise to stay as aware as possible of my unconscious belief systems. I am committed to cracking my emotional and vibrational set points—so I can heal them—and create new, more positive attracting points. I am certain the power to change my life is within me. I believe it is not only possible to change my life—but that I am—regardless of what I have done in the past—or experienced—worthy of abundance in all matters of life. I Am Enough. I Am worthy. I Am connected to all that is. It is my intent, to move beyond any ideas that have me falsely believing that I am in any way a victim. I Am more than what I have been programmed to believe. I Am a creator—and today—no matter where I am—I will make it my primary goal—to stay aware of my emotional set point from moment to moment. From this day forward, I love and accept myself as well as others unconditionally. I surrender to any notion that has me believing any one else owes me anything. I am the master of my destiny—and from this moment on—I am taking ownership over my mind, my unconscious belief systems, my awareness, and my future goals."

CREATING BUILDING BLOCKS FOR YOUR BUSINESS— YOUR NEW LIFE

Once your intent has been outlined in a mission statement, you will have to begin creating building blocks to help you carry through with your desire/vision.

Because the business of changing your life—is primarily rooted in that which is a product of your unconscious mind—it is going to take everything you've got—to maintain a level of awareness—sufficient enough to help you stay emotionally detached from the unconscious beliefs you hold.

Staying AWARE is the key. Without awareness—you cannot change your unconscious belief systems.

How To Stay Aware

> Get regimented. If you do not adopt some type of a regimen, it will be very easy for you to get pulled back into old unconscious thought cycles. Every morning you absolutely must get up at least fifteen minutes earlier than you are used to, and begin journaling about the thoughts that you have caught yourself thinking unconsciously—that were negative in nature.
>
> Begin each morning with the intent to not only uncover some of your unconscious thought patterns, but also begin laying down new, healthier tracks (thought patterns).

A typical morning journal entry might begin like this;

'Yesterday while I was getting into my car, I looked into my rear view mirror and I immediately heard my mind saying, 'Wow you look like crap—You are getting so many wrinkles. I hate the way I look. I hate getting older'. I also noticed how sad I felt the minute I became aware at what my mind was saying. Once I paid attention to what I was saying to myself unconsciously and without even thinking about it, I also noticed the emotions that surfaced as well. They were in total alignment with what my mind was saying unconsciously. I am beginning to understand how synergistic my total being is. I had a thought, and immediately my emotions matched the negative thought. Just a peek into my unconscious mind allowed me to be more aware throughout the day. I was shocked at how many times I caught myself unconsciously thinking negatively about my body, as well as about my ability. Every time I noticed my mind thinking negatively about myself—I could actually feel the energy shift in a negative way within my body. I now understand that—that energy shift—is my point of attraction, and as long as I am aware of my point of attraction at any given moment—I can choose to shift my awareness through the power of focus. Because this is a free will universe—I have the power to think whatever thoughts I want to think—and if I want to—I can at any time—shift my focus to more pleasing thoughts. After noticing my negative self talk—I immediately said 'NO' inside my own brain—and started laying down new positive self talk. Once I noticed how negative my self-talk was, while looking into my rear view mirror, I followed those thoughts with more positive ones. I said to myself, 'Even though I just ripped you apart—I am so sorry I allowed that to happen. I am learning to accept myself—and even my wrinkles. I promise that from

> now I on—I am going to do all I can to fall in love with YOU (me)—and as often as I can—I am going to remind myself to let the negative thinking patterns go, while at same time—learn to accept YOU (me) for who you (we) are. I know I Am a divine being—I know I Am worthy—its just going to take my brain some time to catch up with what my inner being knows to be true. I love you, I accept you, and I am sorry.'

By journaling each morning about the day before, you are cracking your negative emotional codes. It doesn't matter what your basis for negative codes are. The universe doesn't care whether you are the adult child of an alcoholic, or were raised by parents who did not meet your emotional, intellectual, physical or spiritual needs. The universe has no record of why you think poorly about self. It only knows that you do, and therefore—you can only attract more of that which you are at an unconscious level and thus vibrational level. The goal of creating a regimen is to keep momentum flowing within you in a more positive way. Without this type of dedication and commitment to self-awareness—your unconscious mind will take over and your life will play out on autopilot without any real direction from you on a conscious level. And—this will be your choice.

Absorb Yourself With Knowledge

> The more you absorb yourself with this type of information, the more tools you have in your mental shed. Cracking ones own emotional codes is not an easy thing to do. Because the very nature of your perceptions about self, and others, as well as the world is corrupt—it takes an incredible amount of resilience to objectify the thoughts and emotions that you have been building your entire life upon. Coming to terms with the idea that quite possibly everything you once thought about self, others,

life and the world—is wrong—is not only frightening—but sometimes it can be downright overwhelming.

Staying clear about your personal goals is key.

By throwing yourself into seas of information about enlightenment—as well as emotional recovery—is akin to gathering up the troops before heading off into battle. Because very often the people we love are the reasons for why we hate ourselves—it is sometimes necessary to stay away from anyone who might interfere with our ever-growing changing concepts. Because fear based beings fear change, any hint that you might be changing—can cause others to act out—and try and make you doubt self.

Sometimes it is easier to heal alone—than when in the company of others whose agenda it is to not see truth.

Get more comfortable with spending time alone—wrapped up in blankets and surrounded by books, video's and cd's of teachers of enlightenment and emotional recovery.

Part of your regimen must be to find time during your day (perhaps after work or right before bed) to ingest new information about healing and recovery work. Make spending time alone a priority—absorbing new information.

Get To A Meeting

There are a number of free social club organizations that center around helping beings heal from traumas of the past. AA, Al-Anon, CODA, Overeaters Anonymous, Narcotics Anonymous, Gamblers Anonymous and alike are just to name a few.

Most hospitals and YMCA's offer free classes as well as meetings to those in need of emotional support.

Make attending daily or weekly support groups, part of your overall regimen schedule.

Exercise

Your body is synergistically connected to your emotional body, as well as your mental body. Because they are so intertwined, ignoring one—has a negative impact on the whole of your being.

Exercising your physical body enhances the results of the exercising you are doing on the non-physical realm (your emotional self).

Intend to make walking, jogging, stretching, hiking, dancing, or biking a part of your daily regimen.

Meditation

Most beings are unaware at how mindless as well as continuous their streams of thoughts are. To aid one in gaining control over ones mental activity, one must engage in some kind of meditative practice.

Meditation allows the being to slow the mental processes down.

Your brain does not think. It houses the thoughts your mind has been conditioned to think. Your brain is like a motherboard. Your programming is your data. Being raised by dysfunctional caretakers corrupts the data a growing brain receives. It is not easy to wrap your psychological fingers around the idea—that your thoughts are what are wrong. It requires a detached mind to be able to not only 'see' what is corrupt in ones thought process—but to objectify them—and eventually let them go.

Meditation is another secret to your success.

Meditation is like a screwdriver. It helps you get that screw out of the back of that pocket watch so you the watch-master can visually 'see' what might be corrupt in the gears of the watch.

The mind works very much like a delicately layered pocket watch. Every pocket watch has a number of finely tuned gears that need to work synergistically with other gears.

There is no need to go within the heart of a pocket watch—unless of course the pocket watch no longer keeps time.

In order to fix what might be wrong—one would first have to acknowledge that there was something array with his/her watch.

Once you as the watch owner accepted that there was something wrong with the watch—you as the watch master—would go into your bag of tricks and search out for just the appropriately fitting tool that would allow you to look inside the watch for what might be wrong.

You wouldn't take a hammer and slam the back of the watch off—nor would you act as if the watch kept correct time if it didn't. You wouldn't hate the watch, or get angry with the watch. Instead, because you loved the watch, and understood it was not the watch's fault it was having trouble keeping up—

and working as efficiently as it could—you would simply get your tiny screwdriver and unscrew the back of the watch—so you could 'go within' the watch—with the intent of merely fixing what was corrupt.

Imagine if you didn't have that tiny screwdriver.

Imagine if although you knew something was corrupt inside the heart and mind of the watch—you had no clue how to get inside to fix what might be wrong.

Imagine keeping the watch inside your pocket—and knowing you had no other way of telling time.

How might you feel?

You would feel insecure—and perhaps eventually might even get angry and depressed—because not only do you not have the proper tool required to 'see inside' the watch—you don't even know that what's wrong can be fixed—or how to fix it.

Many beings live their lives like owners of broken pocket watches—that do not know their watches are broken—and can be fixed.

Many beings live their lives on auto pilot—operating off of corrupt data, unaware that their haphazard life experiences—are the result of living below a veil of illusion—that prevents them from comprehending just how able they truly are—to correct what is at the heart of their unhealthy life experiences.

Meditation, like the tiny screwdriver used to pop off the back of your pocket watch, is a tool, which allows you to look within at the gears of your own mind.

The purpose of meditation is expansive.

Meditation helps slow down the mind, so one can learn to see just how ones thought process unfolds. Meditation allows beings to become observers of their own minds—which greatly adds to the ability to detach—as well as objectify ones own thought process.

Like watching clouds roll past your field of vision—meditation allows your thoughts to become like passing things—opposed to the grip on your emotional tail.

Because most unaware beings mindlessly react to their emotions—rather than objectify them—or observe them instead—the world is full of people who have no concept of the idea that at any point in time—they have within them the divine ability to become a silent witness—or the observer of their emotions and thought processes—rather than continue to be a slave or a reactor to their emotions—which is the result of faulty programming.

The data that is you—can be corrected.

Meditation is the conduit to the soul.

Choosing not to meditate while on the road to recovery—is like trying to use an ax to pry open the back of that pocket watch.

As you continue to grow in your divine ability to detach and objectify your emotional set points—continued meditation practices allow you to connect even more deeply with the divine aspects of your true nature.

Incorporating daily meditation into your regimen is a must.

Detox

If you have the means possible consider going to a naturopath who can help you come up with a meal plan that is centered upon detoxifying your body of unwanted toxins. The brain is an organ that needs to be fed properly in order to function optimally. If you do not have the means necessary to hire a naturopath do the research yourself. In this day and age most of us have no excuse not to know how our body functions. Technology makes attaining information immediate.

Your body as well as your brain is no one's responsibility but your own.

Most people understand how their cell phones function better than they do cellular metabolism.

Most beings are ignorant to the idea that the 'mind' is a thing that much like a cell phone must be understood in order to get the most out of it. And yet, millions of beings ignore the most powerful computer they will ever own—their brain.

Nutrition

Let's just get over it already. If your diet consists of eggs, cheese, and bacon on a buttered roll for breakfast, a deluxe cheese hamburger and French fries for lunch, and fried fish and buttered mashed potatoes for dinner, do you really believe your body will be able to function optimally?

Your body is your temple, literally. Your blood system is like a river. It transports nutrients to your cells. Insulin is the key that unlocks a cell membrane so that glucose can be converted into energy within the cells.

Overeating and especially overeating heavy fatty and sugary meals is akin to running old, thick oil through your cars engine, while driving 100 miles per hour across the country.

Eventually the pancreas gives out. The pancreas simply cannot keep up with the insulin demands placed on the body, by the amounts of, as well as the types of foods eaten by the being.

Eating poorly poisons your blood system, and makes it very difficult for cells to stay healthy for very long.

Think of your bodies blood system as a polluted river. Now think of your cells as the fish that need to survive in that river. The cleaner the rivers water, the healthier the fish.

If you have the means possible to seek the advice of a nutritionist, or a dietician, and if you are committed to healing from within, then find one in your area you feel comfortable talking to about your needs.

If you do not have the financial means necessary to hire a dietician or nutritionist, then research all you can about how the human body works, and what foods are the healthiest to eat.

Talk It Out

Talk therapy is very helpful as it allows the emotions that have stunted emotional development to finally filter through the emotional, mental and physical planes.

Because abused children often times sadly suffer arrest of emotional development, and are unaware that their decision making and perceptions are being processed through an immature emotional lens, once repressed emotions surface and are permitted to be released while in the presence of an accepting and trusting other—often times wounded beings heal quite quickly.

Today there are a number of options a being can choose from in order to achieve mind, body, and soul integration.

Unlike twenty, thirty or fifty years ago when the only option for emotional help was found through the field of clinical psychiatry, today beings can choose from a wide range of therapeutic options which include professionals who are dedicated to spiritual transcendence.

From Life Coaching, Spiritual Healing, Energy Healing, Reiki Healing, Emotional Release Technicians, Addiction Counselors, Sponsorship, Counseling and alike, today beings have a plethora of options to choose from that are able to enhance ones healing regimen.

LETTING GO

It is my hope that as the teachings of this book come to a close, you my dear reader understand that in order to attract all the things you desire, you must first be in alignment with the things you hear your conscious mind wanting, and that the true secret to manifesting a life worth living lies in how one perceives Self. If others have wounded you in your life, I am sorry. I am sorry that you were not handled with the warmest and the gentlest of hands, hearts or minds. I am sorry that those you loved, may not have loved you the way you deserved to be loved. But I am not sorry your life experience has brought you to the teachings you have found here today.

In life I have discovered that pain has been my greatest motivator, educator, and facilitator of change. Pain, like a double-edged sword destroyed as well as birthed desires within me. Once I catered to beings I wished would validate me. Today however, I no longer crave to be validated or use the tool of caretaking to manipulate others into finding worth in me. The pain of having others withhold their love, approval, understanding, empathy and support from me, at times made me feel like life wasn't worth living. Loving beings that refuse to love me back, was suicidal.

Although being emotionally neglected and rejected nearly destroyed me, at same time many desires, wishes, wants and dreams were being born within me I had no conscious awareness of. It was not until I let go of all of those who harmed me, and embraced falling in love with my own Self, did I even know those new desires had been birthed at all.

Letting go not only relates to the concept of turning away from those who may have harmed us. It also refers to 'letting go or releasing' any dysfunctional ideas we may have adopted along our life's path. It means we learn to face our aloneness—no matter how terrifying. It means we learn to let go of trying to get others to validate us. It means we learn to let go of complaining and whining our ways through life. It means we learn to let go of the labels others gave us as well as those we gave ourselves. It means we stop seeking happiness in things society has brainwashed us to believe will make a man/woman happy. It means we let go of believing that youth, weight, economics, ethnicity, religion, or geography is tied to any sense of self worth. It means we learn to let go of judging others for any reason. It means we learn to let go of judging ourselves. It means we let go of blaming the weather or the news reports about unemployment for our moodiness. It means we learn to let go of placing our unhappiness as well as our happiness on things and or people that exist outside of self.

Dear One, if I could blink my eye and show you just how divine and powerful you are, I wouldn't.

There is no greater accomplishment than the accomplishment over ones false ideas about Self.

You are on the road to victory, and no one deserves the glory of triumph over tragedy but you.

Enjoy the ride.

Namaste…

Lisa